TUNING THE GU

M000169277

The six open strings of the guitar will be of the same pitch as the six notes shown in the illustration of the piano keyboard. Note that five of the strings are below the middle C of the piano keyboard.

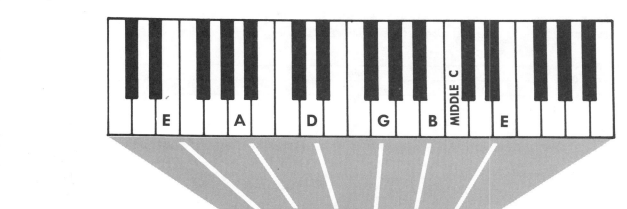

PIANO NOTATION

E A D G B E

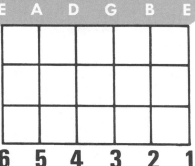

6 5 4 3 2 1

GUITAR NOTATION

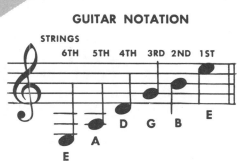

ANOTHER METHOD OF TUNING

1. Tune the 6th string in unison to the **E** or twelfth white key to the LEFT of MIDDLE C on the piano.

2. Place the finger behind the fifth fret of the 6th string. This will give you the tone or pitch of the 5th string. (**A**)

3. Place finger behind the fifth fret of the 5th string to get the pitch of the 4th string. (**D**)

4. Repeat same procedure to obtain the pitch of the 3rd string. (**G**)

5. Place finger behind the FOURTH FRET of the 3rd string to get the pitch of the 2nd string. (**B**)

6. Place finger behind the fifth fret of the 2nd string to get the pitch of the 1st string. (**E**)

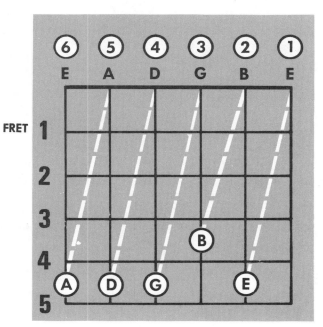

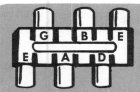

PITCH PIPES

Pitch pipes with instructions for their usage may be obtained at any music store. Each pipe will have the correct pitch of each guitar string and are recommended to be used when a piano is not available.

THE RUDIMENTS OF MUSIC

THE STAFF: Music is written on a STAFF consisting of FIVE LINES and FOUR SPACES. The lines and spaces are numbered upward as shown:

5TH LINE
4TH LINE   4TH SPACE
3RD LINE   3RD SPACE
2ND LINE   2ND SPACE
1ST LINE   1ST SPACE

THE LINES AND SPACES ARE NAMED AFTER LETTERS OF THE ALPHABET.

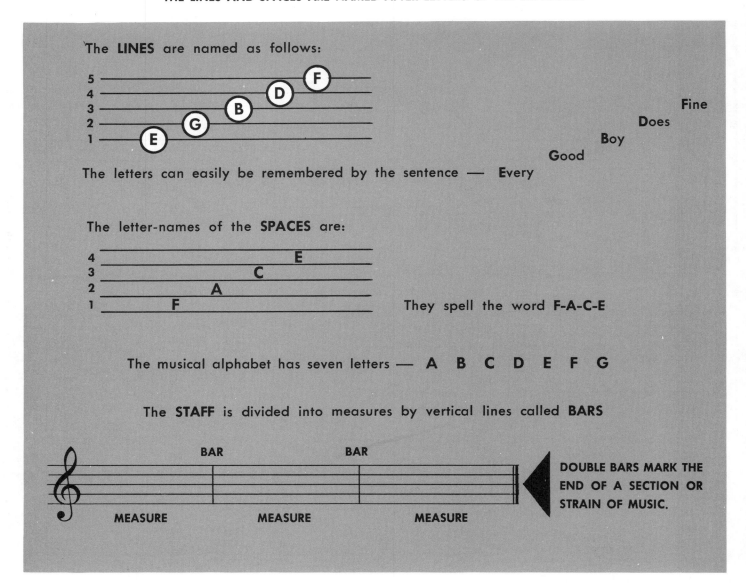

The **LINES** are named as follows:

5 — F
4 — D
3 — B
2 — G
1 — E

The letters can easily be remembered by the sentence — Every Good Boy Does Fine

The letter-names of the **SPACES** are:

4 — E
3 — C
2 — A
1 — F

They spell the word **F-A-C-E**

The musical alphabet has seven letters — **A B C D E F G**

The **STAFF** is divided into measures by vertical lines called **BARS**

BAR   BAR

MEASURE   MEASURE   MEASURE

DOUBLE BARS MARK THE END OF A SECTION OR STRAIN OF MUSIC.

THE CLEF:

THIS SIGN IS THE TREBLE OR G CLEF.

ALL GUITAR MUSIC WILL BE WRITTEN IN THIS CLEF.

THE SECOND LINE OF THE TREBLE CLEF IS KNOWN AS THE G LINE. MANY PEOPLE CALL THE TREBLE CLEF THE G CLEF BECAUSE IT CIRCLES AROUND THE G LINE.

MEL BAY'S COMPLETE METHOD FOR CLASSIC GUITAR

By Mel Bay

This book contains a wealth of technical studies, right-hand exercises, music theory, and music from the masters. Selections from such greats as Sor, Tarrega, Aguado, Carcassi, Bach, and others were carefully selected, edited, and arranged in varying levels of difficulty. Now for the first time we present, under one cover, the **Complete Mel Bay Method for Classic Guitar.**

Guitar on cover hand-crafted by Pimentel & Sons, Albuquerque, New Mexico.

Copyright © 1976 by Mel Bay Publications, Inc., Pacific, MO 63069.
International Copyright Secured. All Rights Reserved. Printed in U.S.A.

2

REQUIRED SUPPLEMENTS

1.	EASY CLASSIC SOLOS	—	Easy Solos
2.	GREAT CLASSIC SOLOS	—	Intermediate
3.	DELUXE ALBUM OF CLASSICAL GUITAR MUSIC	—	Advanced
4.	FLAMENCO GUITAR	—	Intermediate
5.	DELUXE GUITAR SCALE BOOK	—	Theory
6.	SOLO FOLIO #1	—	Easy
7.	GUITAR TECHNIC	—	Technic
8.	GUITAR FINGERBOARD HARMONY	—	Theory
9.	GUITAR ARPEGGIO STUDIES	—	Technic
10.	GUITAR ENSEMBLES	—	Quartets
11.	GUITAR DUETS ON GREAT CLASSIC THEMES	—	Duets
12.	SACRED GUITARIST	—	Solos
13.	GOSPEL GUITAR	—	Solos

MEL BAY PUBLICATIONS • **PACIFIC, MISSOURI 63069**

©Copyright 1976 by Mel Bay Publications, Inc., Pacific, Mo.
International Copyright Secured -:- All Rights Reserved -:- Printed in U.S.A.

NOTES:

THIS IS A NOTE:

A NOTE HAS THREE PARTS. THEY ARE

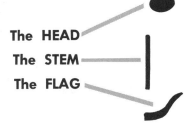

The HEAD
The STEM
The FLAG

NOTES MAY BE PLACED IN THE STAFF, ABOVE THE STAFF,

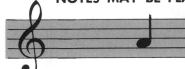  

AND BELOW THE STAFF.

A note will bear the name of the line or space it occupies on the staff.

The location of a note in, above or below the staff will indicate the Pitch.

PITCH: the highness or lowness of a tone.

TONE: a musical sound.

TYPES OF NOTES

THE TYPE OF NOTE WILL INDICATE THE LENGTH OF ITS SOUND.

THIS IS A WHOLE NOTE. THE HEAD IS HOLLOW. IT DOES NOT HAVE A STEM.

= 4 BEATS
A WHOLE-NOTE WILL RECEIVE FOUR BEATS OR COUNTS.

THIS IS A HALF NOTE THE HEAD IS HOLLOW. IT HAS A STEM.

= 2 BEATS
A HALF-NOTE WILL RECEIVE TWO BEATS OR COUNTS.

THIS IS A QUARTER NOTE THE HEAD IS SOLID. IT HAS A STEM.

= 1 BEAT
A QUARTER NOTE WILL RECEIVE ONE BEAT OR COUNT.

THIS IS AN EIGHTH NOTE THE HEAD IS SOLID. IT HAS A STEM AND A FLAG.

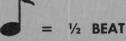 = ½ BEAT
AN EIGHTH-NOTE WILL RECEIVE ONE-HALF BEAT OR COUNT. (2 FOR 1 BEAT)

RESTS:

A REST is a sign used to designate a period of silence.

This period of silence will be of the same duration of time as the note to which it corresponds.

  THIS IS AN EIGHTH REST

  THIS IS A QUARTER REST

 THIS IS A HALF REST. NOTE THAT IT LAYS ON THE LINE.

 THIS IS A WHOLE REST. NOTE THAT IT HANGS DOWN FROM THE LINE.

NOTES

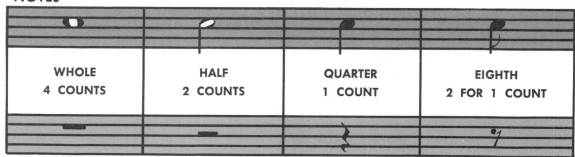

WHOLE 4 COUNTS	HALF 2 COUNTS	QUARTER 1 COUNT	EIGHTH 2 FOR 1 COUNT

RESTS

THE TIME SIGNATURE

THE ABOVE EXAMPLES ARE THE COMMON TYPES OF TIME SIGNATURES TO BE USED IN THIS BOOK.

4 THE TOP NUMBER INDICATES THE NUMBER OF BEATS PER MEASURE.

4 THE BOTTOM NUMBER INDICATES THE TYPE OF NOTE RECEIVING ONE BEAT.

4 BEATS PER MEASURE

4 A QUARTER-NOTE RECEIVES ONE BEAT

 SIGNIFIES SO CALLED "COMMON TIME" AND IS SIMPLY ANOTHER WAY OF DESIGNATING 4/4 TIME.

LEDGER LINES:

When the pitch of a musical sound is below or above the staff, the notes are then placed on, or between, extra lines called LEDGER LINES.

THEY WILL BE LIKE THIS:

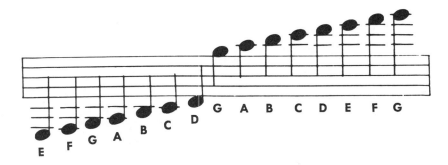

E F G A B C D G A B C D E F G

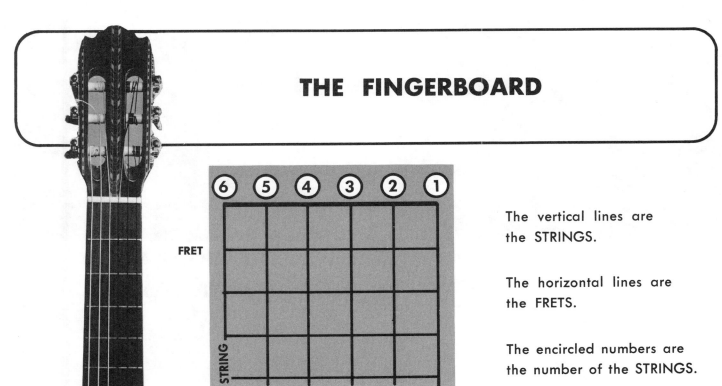

THE FINGERBOARD

The vertical lines are the STRINGS.

The horizontal lines are the FRETS.

The encircled numbers are the number of the STRINGS.

STRING-NUMBERS: The encircled numbers **6 5 4 3 2 1** will be the numbers of the STRINGS.

CHARTS:

The charts used in this book will have the VERTICAL-LINES as the STRINGS and the HORIZONTAL-LINES as the FRETS.

Reading from left to right the strings will be: ⑥ ⑤ ④ ③ ② ①

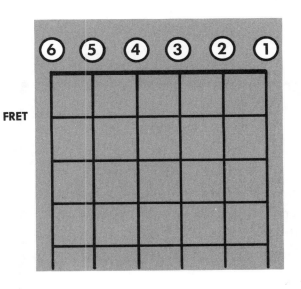

The Correct Way To Hold the Guitar
(TWO WAYS SHOWN)

1. The Left Leg Crossed over the Right.

2. Placing the Left Foot on a Small Stool.

THE RIGHT HAND
(R. H.)

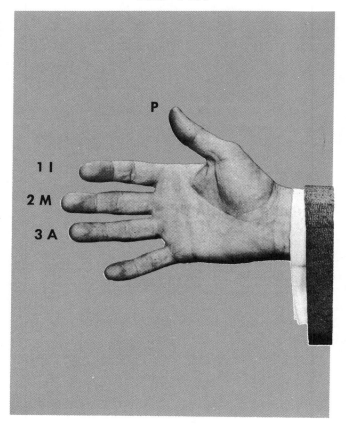

THE RIGHT HAND FINGERS WILL BE DESIGNATED AS

1 = I

2 = M

3 = A

Thumb = P

THE NAMES OF THE R. H. FINGERS ARE:

(English)	(ABV)	(Spanish)
1st — Index	(I)	Indice
2nd — Middle	(M)	Medio
3rd — Ring	(A)	Anular
Thumb —	(P)	Pulgar

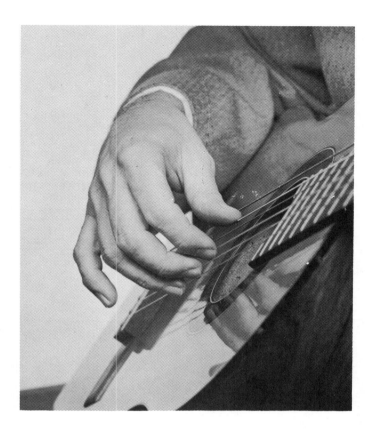

THE LEFT HAND
(L. H.)

The Left Hand Position

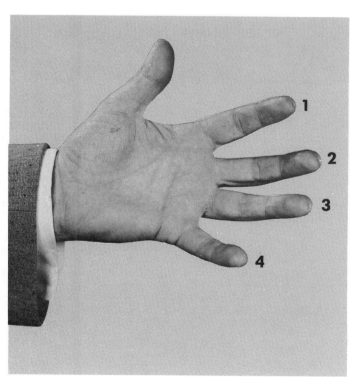

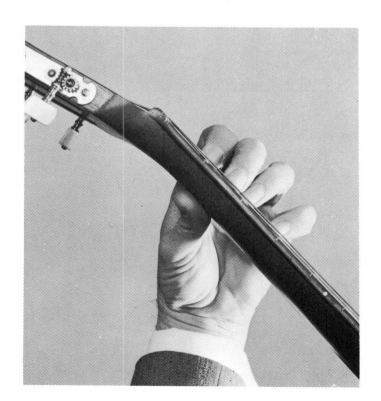

Place your fingers **firmly** on the strings **directly behind** the frets.

NOTES ON THE FIRST STRING

Classic G. M. 1

NOTES ON THE SECOND STRING

THREE NOTES ON THE 2ND STRING

B C D

(OPEN) 1ST FRET 3RD FRET
1ST FINGER 3RD FINGER

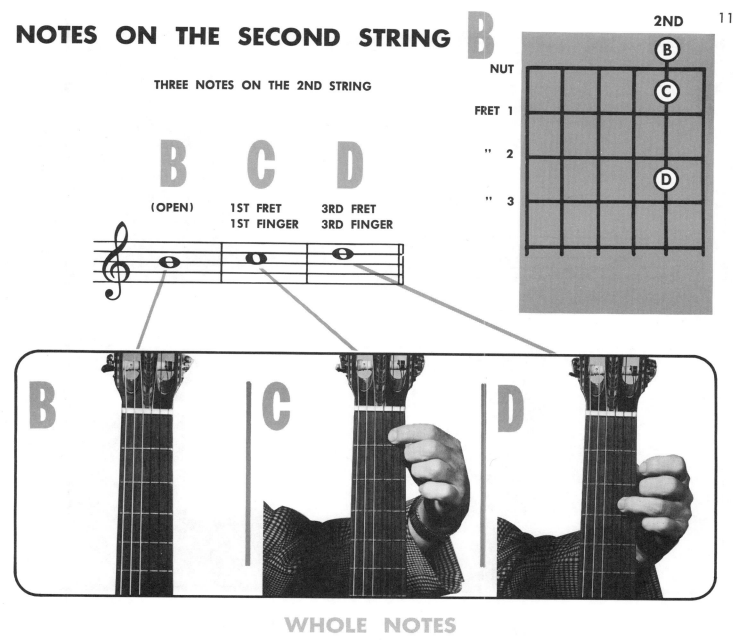

WHOLE NOTES

COUNT: 1 2 3 4

HALF NOTES

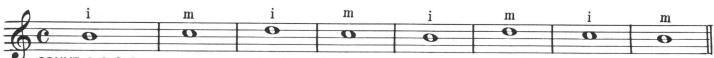

COUNT: 1 2 3 4

QUARTER NOTES

COUNT: 1 2 3 4

NOTES ON THE THIRD STRING G

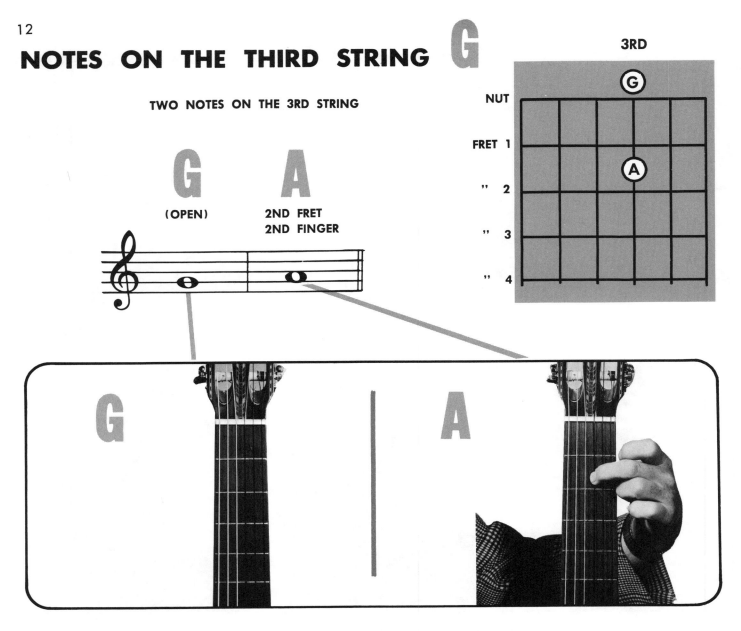

TWO NOTES ON THE 3RD STRING

G (OPEN)

A 2ND FRET 2ND FINGER

3RD

NUT

FRET 1

" 2

" 3

" 4

G

A

A STUDY ON THE THIRD STRING

COUNT: 1 2 3 4

Sparkling Stella

Right Hand Study

Repeat the above study until mastered.

Introducing the Right Hand Third Finger (a)

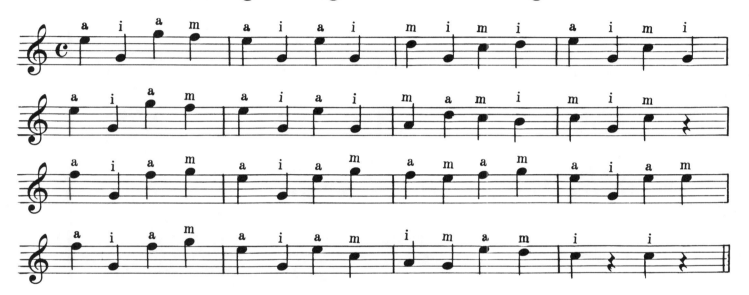

THREE-FOUR TIME

This sign  indicates THREE-FOUR time.

3 — BEATS PER MEASURE.
4 — TYPE OF NOTE RECEIVING ONE BEAT (quarter note).

In THREE-FOUR time, we will have three beats per measure.

DOTTED HALF NOTES

A dot (•) placed behind a note increases its value by one-half.

A dotted half-note (𝅗𝅥•) will receive three beats.

𝅗𝅥 = 2 COUNTS   𝅗𝅥• = 3 COUNTS

The Merry Men

NOTES ON THE FOURTH STRING D

THREE NOTES ON THE 4TH STRING

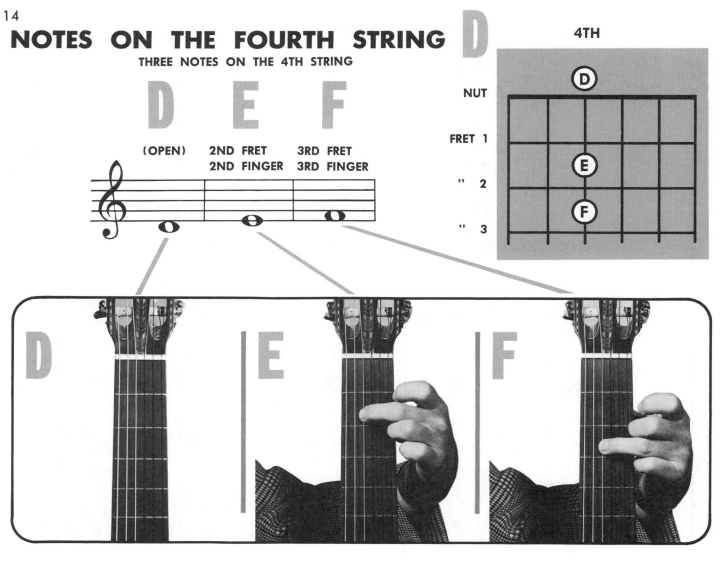

WHOLE NOTES

COUNT: 1 2 3 4

HALF NOTES

COUNT: 1 2 3 4   1 2 (3 4)

QUARTER NOTES

COUNT: 1 2 3 4   1 2 3 (4)

NOTES ON THE FIFTH STRING A

THREE NOTES ON THE 5TH STRING

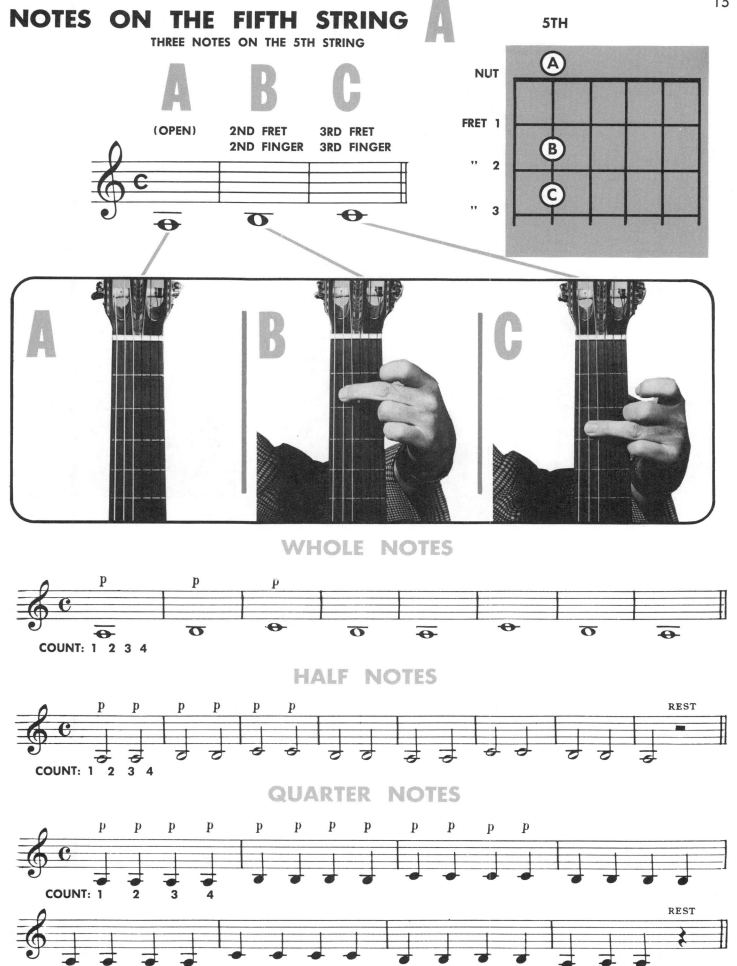

WHOLE NOTES

COUNT: 1 2 3 4

HALF NOTES

COUNT: 1 2 3 4

QUARTER NOTES

COUNT: 1 2 3 4

NOTES ON THE SIXTH STRING
THREE NOTES ON THE 6TH STRING

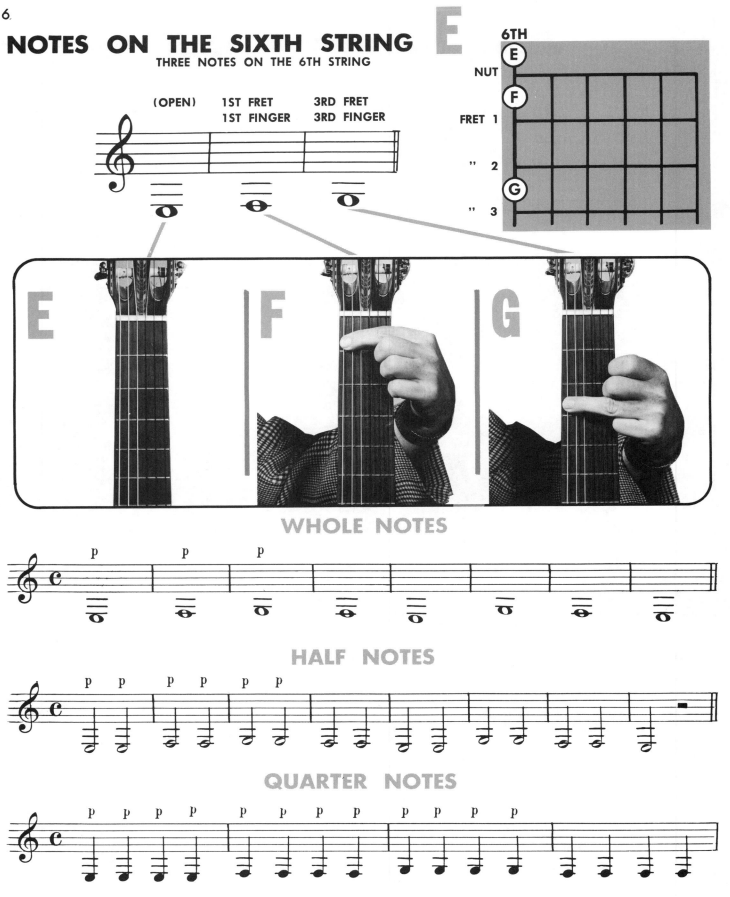

WHOLE NOTES

HALF NOTES

QUARTER NOTES

Two Solos

The following solos will be played on the 6th, 5th, and 4th strings.

Play slowly at first keeping the time as evenly as possible.

Do not raise the left hand fingers from the strings until absolutely necessary.

How Can I Leave Thee

Adantino

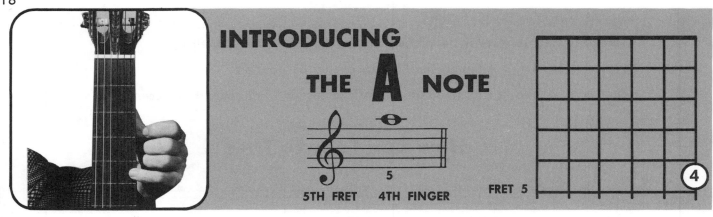

INTRODUCING THE A NOTE

5TH FRET 4TH FINGER

FRET 5

The First String Waltz

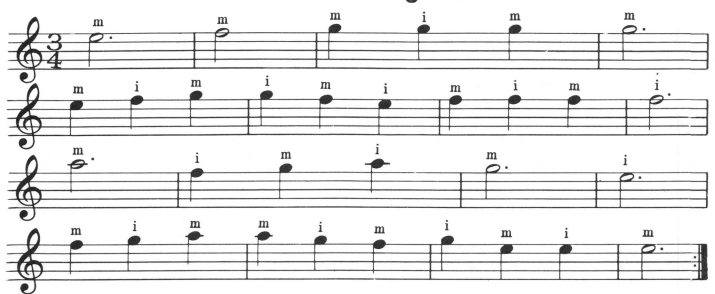

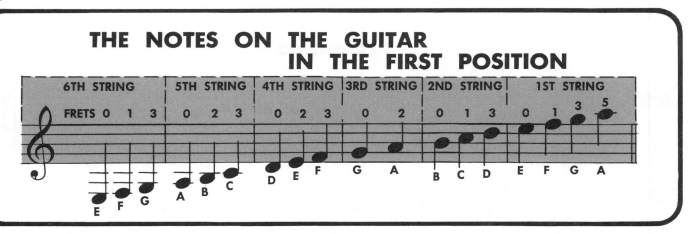

Sixpence

PICK-UP NOTES

One or more notes at the beginning of a strain before the first measure are referred to as pick-up notes.

The rhythm for pick-up notes is taken from the last measure of the selection and the beats are counted as such. Note the three beats in the last measure of the following study.

A Study Introducing the Pick-up Note

Etude

A Study By Aguado

WHEN TWO OR MORE NOTES ARE WRITTEN ON THE SAME STEM PLAY THEM AS ONE.

Example

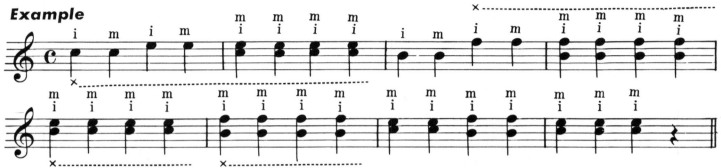

(x---------): Hold L. H. finger down. Never raise fingers until necessary.

In the above Example, play the double notes with the first finger of the R. H., plucking the lower note, and the second finger of the R. H. plucking the top note.

In the following Studies, play the lower notes with the R. H. Thumb (P).

Watch the L. H. fingering.

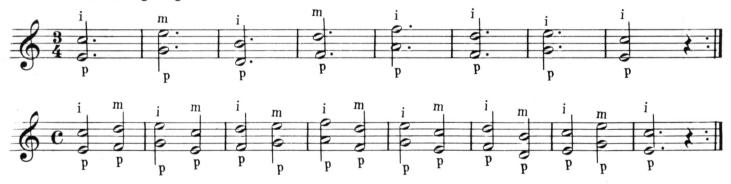

Play the Lower Notes with the Thumb (P)

Repeat the top notes as follows: mimi, mama and amam.

Follow the Leader

Mel Bay

In the following Studies, play the lower notes with the Right Hand Thumb.

Watch the Left Hand fingering.

Alpine Echoes

Mel Bay

Waltz

Mel Bay

See Mel Bay's
''Easy Classic Guitar Solos''

In the following studies the lower notes are played with the thumb.

Hold each note for its full time value.

A Study

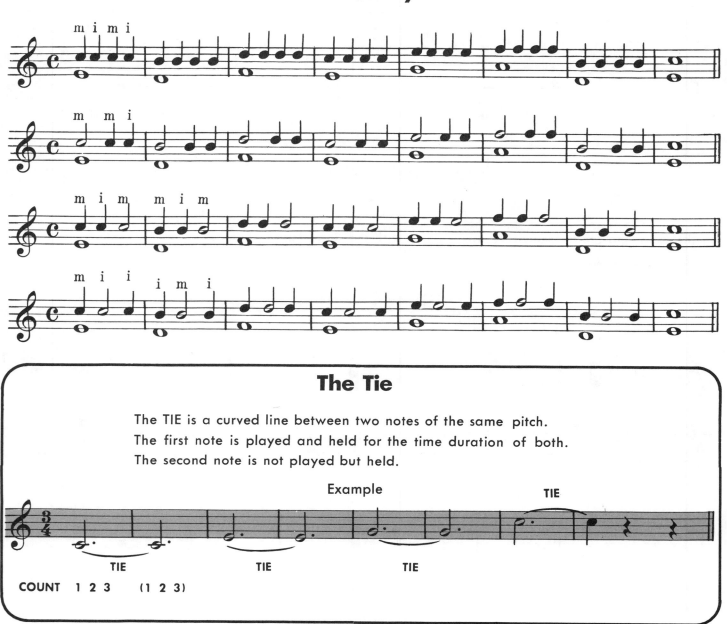

The Tie

The TIE is a curved line between two notes of the same pitch.
The first note is played and held for the time duration of both.
The second note is not played but held.

Example

The Tie Waltz

CHORDS

A MELODY is a succession of single tones.

A CHORD is a combination of tones sounded together.

TONES IN A MELODY.   THE SAME TONES AS A CHORD.

We will construct our chords by playing the chordal tones separately as in a melody and **without raising the fingers**, striking them together.

The Chord Waltz

MEL BAY

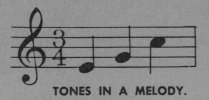

The Builder

MEL BAY

Small Chord Etude

MEL BAY

/ / / = REPEAT CHORD

Practice the above etude until it can be played without missing a beat.

*Note that the first finger holds down two notes (C-F) in the second chord.

Bass Solos With Chord Accompaniment

When playing bass solos with chord accompaniment you will find the solo with the stems turned **downward** and the accompaniment with the stems turned **upward.**

Unless otherwise shown, **play the bass with the R. H. Thumb and the chords with the R. H. 1st, 2nd, and third fingers.**

Example

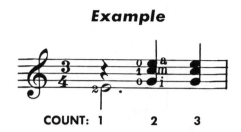

COUNT: 1   2   3

In the example shown above you see the dotted half-note (E) with the stem downward. It is played on the count of **one** and is **held** for counts **two** and **three.**

The quarter rest over the dotted half-note indicates that there is **no chord accompaniment at the count of one.** The chords with the stems upward are played on counts of **two** and **three.**

Bass Solo With Chord Accompaniment

MEL BAY

Little Minuet

Adaptation of a
melody by CARCASSI

CHORDS IN THE KEY OF C MAJOR

The key of C has three principal chords. They are C, F, and G7.

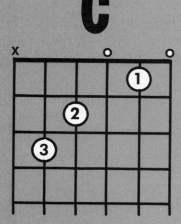
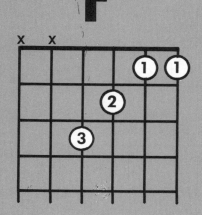
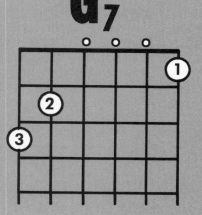

The circles indicate the positions to place your fingers.

Numerals inside circles indicate the fingers.

(x) over the strings means that the strings are **not** to be played.

(o) over the strings indicates the strings to be played open.

Place fingers on positions indicated by the circles and strike them all together.

Musical Notation of the Chords

Accompaniment Styles

Alternate Basses

In Three-Four Time

THE KEY OF C
All music studied so far in this book has been in the Key of C.

That means that the notes have been taken from the C Scale (shown at right) and made into melodies.

It is called the C Scale because the first note is C and we proceed through the musical alphabet until C reappears. C-D-E-F-G-A-B-C.

We will cover the subject of keys and scales more thoroughly in the Theory and Harmony Chapters appearing later on in this course.

At present we will deal only with basic fundamentals.

THE C SCALE

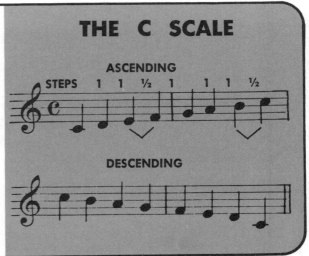

STEPS

A Half-Step is the distance from a given tone to the next higher or lower tone. On the Guitar the distance of a Half-Step is ONE FRET.

A Whole-Step consists of TWO Half-Steps.

The distance of a Whole-Step on the Guitar is TWO FRETS.

The C Scale has two half-steps. They are between E-F and B-C.

Note the distance of one fret between those notes. The distances between C-D, D-E, F-G, G-A, and A-B are Whole-Steps.

Whole-Steps and Half-Steps are also referred to as Whole-Tones and Half-Tones. We will refer to them as Whole-Steps and Half-Steps.

CHROMATICS

The alteration of the pitches of tones is brought about by the use of symbols called CHROMATICS. (Also referred to as ACCIDENTALS)

The Sharp ♯ THE SHARP PLACED BEFORE A NOTE RAISES ITS PITCH ½-STEP OR ONE FRET.

The Flat ♭ THE FLAT PLACED BEFORE A NOTE LOWERS ITS PITCH ½-STEP OR ONE FRET.

The Natural ♮ THE NATURAL RESTORES A NOTE TO ITS NORMAL POSITION. IT CANCELS ALL ACCIDENTALS PREVIOUSLY USED.

Tempo

Tempo is the **rate of speed** of a musical composition.

Three types of tempo used in this book will be:

ANDANTE: A slow easy pace.   MODERATO: Moderate.   ALLEGRO: Lively.

In the following selections pluck the notes with the downward stems with the thumb. Play the top notes as indicated.

Minuetto

GEBAUR, Opus 10
Arr. by MEL BAY

Moderato

Dawn

MAZAS-BAY

Moderato

See Mel Bay's

"Guitar Technique"

THE EIGHTH NOTE

An eighth note receives one-half beat. (One quarter note equals two eighth notes).

An eighth note will have a head, stem, and flag. If two or more are in successive order they may be connected by a bar. (See Example).

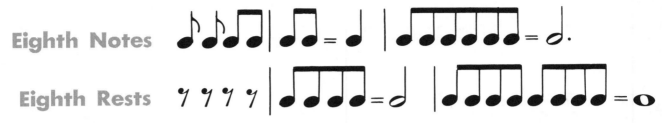

Eighth Notes

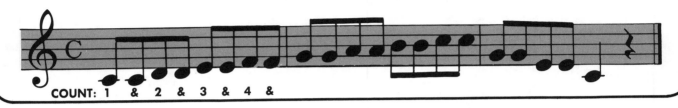

Eighth Rests

The Scale In Eighth Notes

COUNT: 1 & 2 & 3 & 4 &

A Daily Scale Study

MEL BAY

COUNT: 1 & 2 & 3 & 4 &

The above study should be played slowly with a gradual increase of speed until a moderate tempo has been reached. It is an excellent daily exercise.

A Study In Eights

THE KEY OF A MINOR
(Relative to C Major)

Each Major key will have a Relative Minor key.

The Relative Minor Scale is built upon the **sixth tone** of the Major Scale.

The Key Signature of both will be the same.

The Minor Scale will have the same number of tones (7) as the Major.

The difference between the two scales is the arrangement of the whole-steps and half-steps.

There are **three forms** of the minor scale: 1. PURE or NATURAL, 2. HARMONIC, 3. MELODIC.

The A Minor Scale
Natural (Pure)

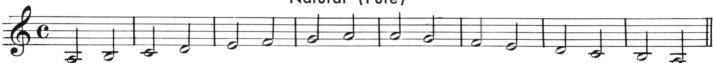

Harmonic

The 7th tone is raised one half-step ascending and descending.

Melodic

The 6th and 7th tones are raised one half-step ascending and lowered back to their normal pitch descending.

A Visit to the Relatives

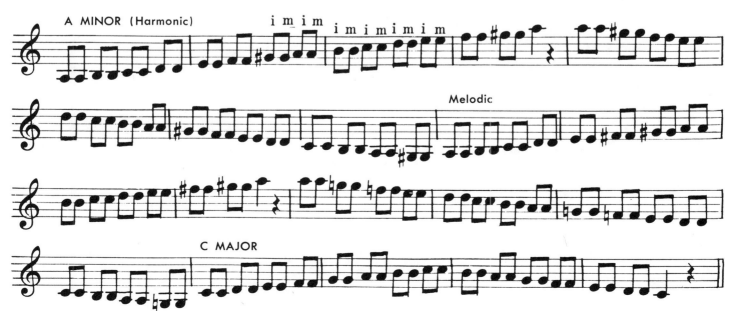

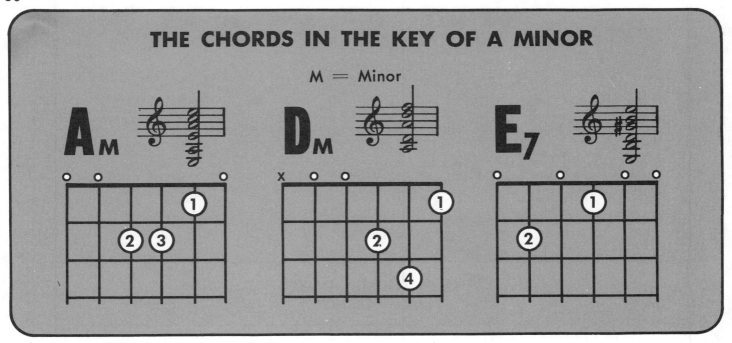

THE CHORDS IN THE KEY OF A MINOR

M = Minor

Accompaniment Styles in A Minor

This sign **%** indicates that the previous measure is to be repeated.

In the following study hold the chords as indicated, playing the melody from those chords.

Etude

Waltz

CARULLI

Playtime

PLEYEL
Arr. by MEL BAY

Moderato

Balkan Nights

MEL BAY

Moderato

A Daily Scale Study in A Minor

Rain Drops

First and Second Endings

Sometimes two endings are required in certain selections . . one to lead back into a repeated chords and one to close it.

They will be shown like this:

The first time play the bracketed ending 1. Repeat the chorus.

The second time skip the first ending and play ending No. 2.

Cradle Song

JOHANN BRAHMS
Arr. by MEL BAY

Right Hand Study

Finger Gymnastics

The following exercises have a two-fold purpose.

(1) Training the individual fingers to perform independently of each other.

(2) Acquainting the student with the technic of position playing that will be an important part of this course.

The first finger should be held down throughout these exercises.

Repeat the above Gymnastics using the following R. H. Patterns:

① — m i m i m i m i ② — m a m a m a m a ③ — a m a m a m a m

The Blue Tail Fly

Arr. by MEL BAY

Right Hand Studies

REPEAT EACH OF THE ABOVE STUDIES UNTIL MASTERED.

Italian Air

Andantino

CARCASSI

Classic Dance

Andantino

MEL BAY

FINE

D. C. al Fine

Da Capo al Fine (D.C. al Fine): Go back to the beginning and play to FINE. (The End)

Other Tempo Terms

ALLEGRETTO . . . . Lively

VIVANCE . . . . Very Fast

PRESTO . . . . As fast as possible

ALLEGRO MODERATO . . . . Moderately fast

ADAGIO . . . . Slower than Andante

ANDANTINO . . . . Faster than Andante

LARGO . . . . Slower than Adagio

LENTO . . . . As slow as possible

Play the RIGHT HAND DEVELOPMENT ETUDE using each of the Six Patterns throughout the entire number.

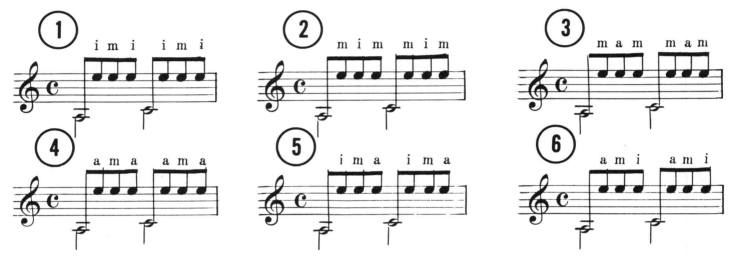

Right Hand Development Etude

See the "MEL BAY FOLIO OF CLASSIC GUITAR SOLOS"

The following Solo introduces the notes D and B being played together. This is 37 done by playing the note D with the first finger on the third fret of the second string and playing the note B with the second finger upon the fourth fret of the THIRD STRING. For two-four time explanation see page 6.

Senorita

Senora

See the "MEL BAY FOLIO OF CLASSIC GUITAR SOLOS"

ANDANTE

F. CARULLI

The Key of G

The Key of G will have one sharp. (F♯)

It will be identified by this signature:

The F-notes will be played as shown:

2nd fret
2nd finger

4th fret
4th finger

2nd fret
2nd finger

The G Scale

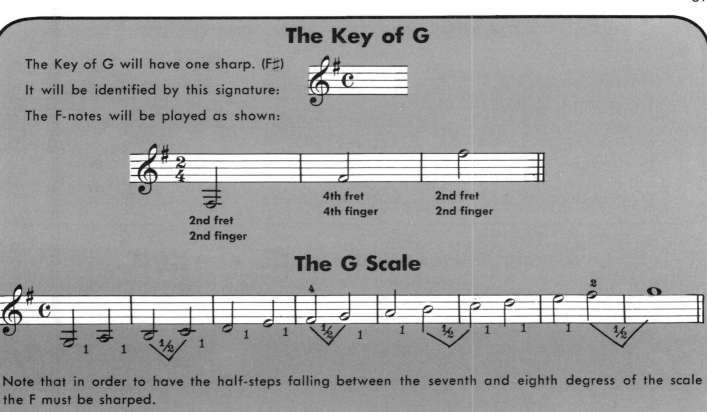

Note that in order to have the half-steps falling between the seventh and eighth degress of the scale the F must be sharped.

Our major scale pattern is then correct. (1, 1, ½, 1, 1, 1, ½.) (steps)

A Daily Drill

The Gauchos

GUITAR SOLO
Allegro

CARCASSI-BAY

CHORDS IN THE KEY OF G

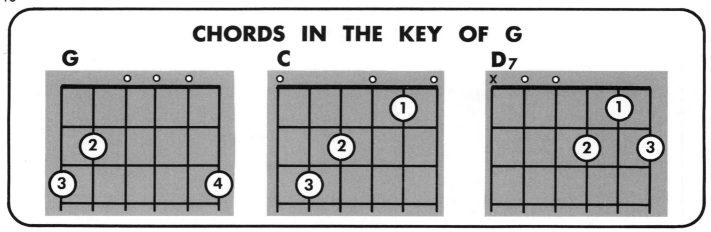

G   C   D7

Accompaniment Styles In The Key Of G

A Scale Study

COUNT: 1 2 & 3 & 4 &

A Serenade

Moderato

MEL BAY

* Three lower notes plucked with the thumb

Austrian Hymn

HAYDN
Arr. by MEL BAY

42

The Little Prince

MAZAS
Arr. by MEL BAY

In the Evening By the Moonlight

BLAND
Arr. by MEL BAY

See the "MEL BAY FOLIO OF CLASSIC GUITAR SOLOS"

THE KEY OF E MINOR

(Relative to G Major)

The Key of E Minor will have the same key signature as G Major.

Two E Minor Scales

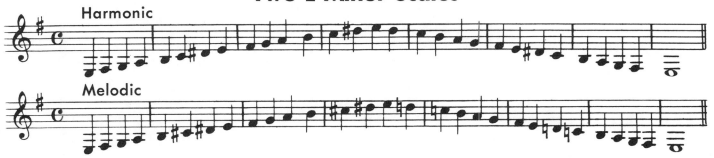

Harmonic

Melodic

The above scales should be memorized.

THE CHORDS IN THE KEY OF E MINOR

The Chords in the Key of E Minor are:

Em   Am   B7

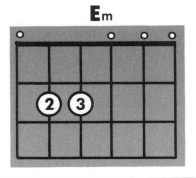   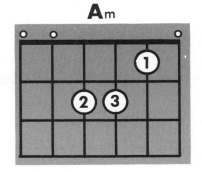   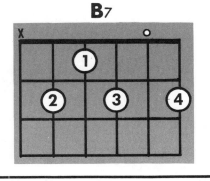

Accompaniment Styles in the Key of E Minor

Dotted Quarter Notes

A DOT AFTER A NOTE increases its Value by ONE-HALF.

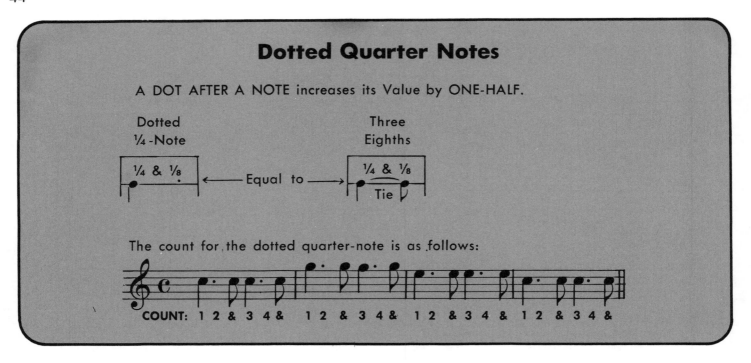

The count for the dotted quarter-note is as follows:

COUNT: 1 2 & 3 4 &   1 2 & 3 4 &   1 2 & 3 4 &   1 2 & 3 4 &

A Dotted Quarter-Note Etude

Right Hand Technique

Hold third finger on the D note throughout.

The Foggy, Foggy Dew

Arr. by MEL BAY

See Mel Bay's

"Deluxe Guitar Scale Book"

A Waltz By Sor

ANDANTE

I. K. MERTZ

A Night In Madrid

A Song By Aguado

Waltz in E Minor

Conchita

AGUADO

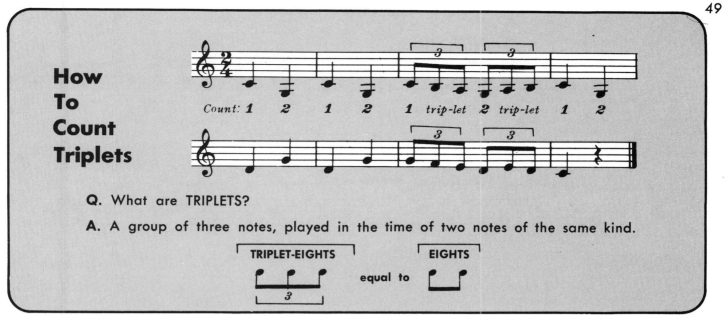

How To Count Triplets

Q. What are TRIPLETS?

A. A group of three notes, played in the time of two notes of the same kind.

TRIPLET-EIGHTS   equal to   EIGHTS

Play the following Triplet Etudes using the following R.H. fingering. pim, pmi, pma, pam.

TRIPLETS

Around the Samovar

Right Hand Triplet Etude

REPEAT UNTIL MASTERED

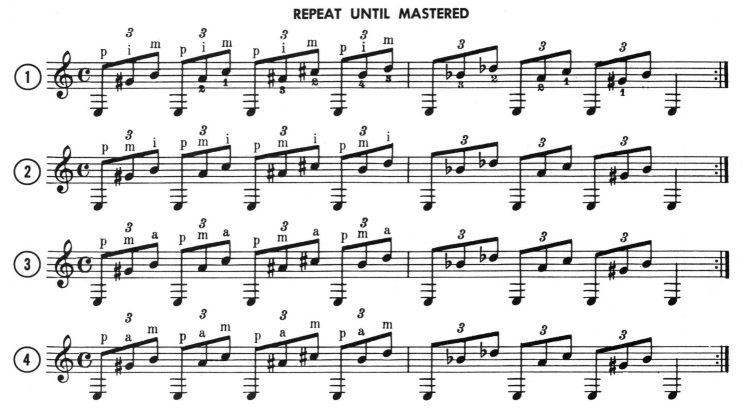

See the "MEL BAY FOLIO OF CLASSIC GUITAR SOLOS"

MODERATO

MAURO GIULIANI

51

Another Triplet Etude

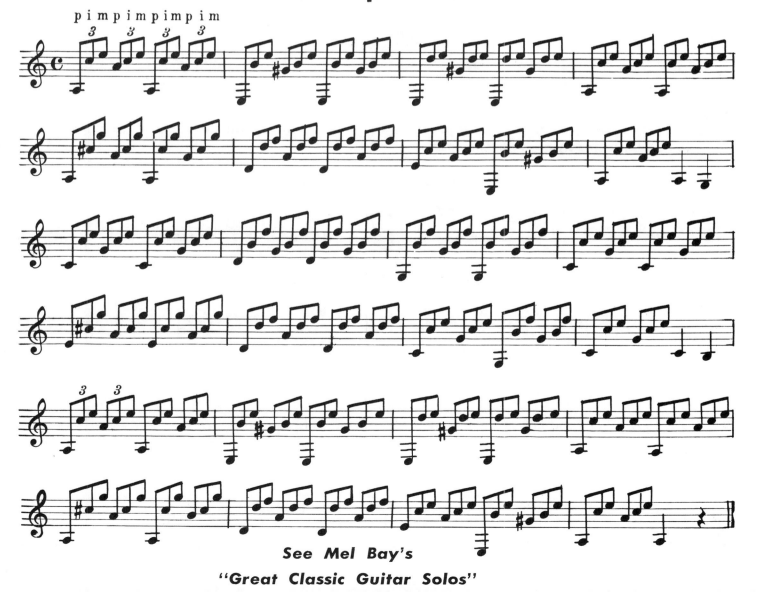

See Mel Bay's

"Great Classic Guitar Solos"

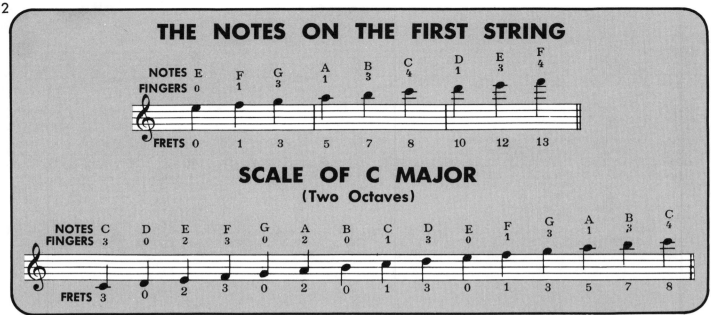

THE SLIDE

The SLIDE is performed by one finger of the left hand sliding over the frets from the first to the second note. The first note is struck and the second note is sounded by the slide.

The slide is indicated by the following sign:

THE SLUR

To execute ascending slurs of two notes, the lower note is to be played and the finger of the left hand descends hammer-like upon the higher note creating the tone desired.

Descending slurs are executed by first fingering the notes to be played with the left hand. Strike the higher note and by drawing the finger sideways off the string, the lower note will automatically sound. Slurred notes will be connected by a curved line. (⌒)

ASCENDING SLURS

DESCENDING SLURS

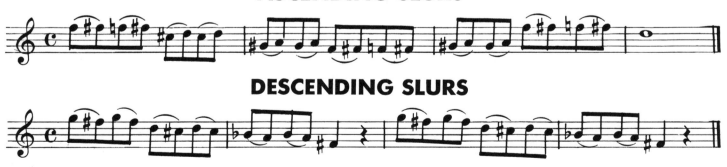

THE SNAP

The SNAP is similiar to the slur in execution. The second note of the SNAP will usually be an open string.

The first note is played and immediately the left hand finger pulls the string sideways as it slides off the fingerboard.

When snapping a note to a closed note, both notes should be held before executing the snap effect.

THE NOTES ON THE SECOND STRING

Shown below are the notes on the second string.

Any note played upon the first string may be played upon the second string **five frets higher** than it's location on the first string.

In the following diagram you will see the notes on the first string and directly below the same notes as played upon the second string. This is a very good aid in remembering the notes on the second string.

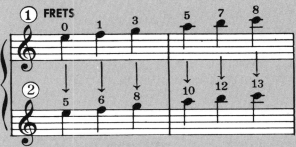

THE C SCALE IN THIRDS

The following study should be played upon the first and second strings.

The **top-note will be on the first string** and the **bottom-note on the second.**

To facilitate execution, it is better to let the fingers remain upon the strings as much as possible, gliding from fret to fret.

Carefully observe the fingering.

An Exercise In Thirds

THE NOTES ON THE FIFTH FRET

THE THIRDS IN THE KEY OF G

Granada Memories
(Based upon an etude by Aguado)

GUITAR SOLO
Moderato

MEL BAY

In the above selection employ the R.H. pattern (Pi Pm) throughout except where otherwise shown.

SIXTEENTH-NOTES

In common time four sixteenth-notes equal one quarter-note.

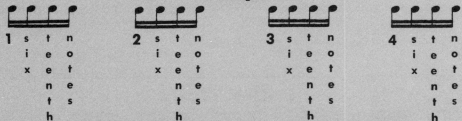

They may be counted in this manner:

1-six-teenth-notes, 2-six-teenth-notes, 3-six-teenth-notes, 4-six-teenth-notes.

Example

TABLE OF NOTES AND RESTS

Whole Note		A Whole Measure Rest	
Half Notes		A Half Rest	
Quarter Notes		A Quarter Rest	
Eighth Notes		An Eighth Rest	
Sixteenth Notes		A Sixteenth Rest	

In the fifth and ninth measures of the following study an eighth note is followed by two sixteenth notes. ()

They may be counted in this manner: 1 & a 2 & a 3 & a 4 & a

Sixteenth-Notes

Repeat the above using the following R.H. Fingers: ①pmim, ②pmam, ③pama, ④pima, ⑤pami

Prelude

THREE-EIGHT TIME

This sign $\begin{array}{c}3\\8\end{array}$ indicates three-eight time.

3 — — beats per measure.

8 — — type of note receiving one beat. (eight note)

An eighth-note ♪ = one beat, a quarter-note ♩ = two beats and a dotted quarter-note

♩· = three beats. A sixteenth-note ♬ = ½ beat.

Petite Waltz

Carcassi's Waltz

THE KEY OF D MAJOR

The Key of D Major will have two sharps—F♯ and C♯.

To facilitate the fingering in the Key of D Major, it is necessary to move the first finger to the second fret, the second finger to the third fret and the third finger to the fourth fret. (Note scale)

THE D MAJOR SCALE

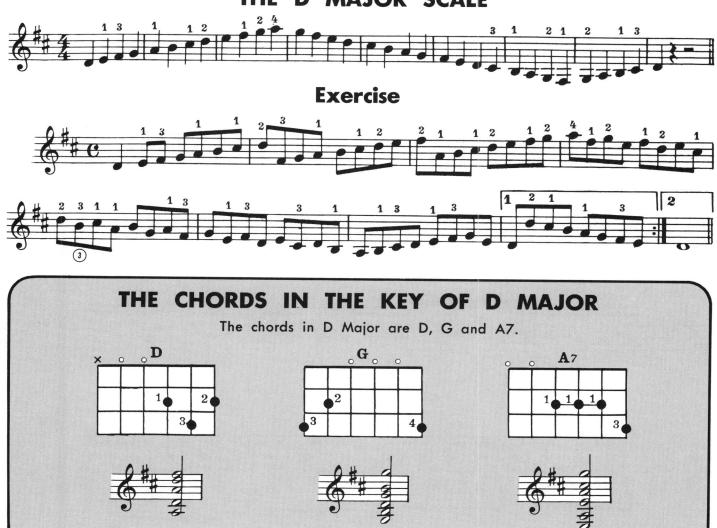

Exercise

THE CHORDS IN THE KEY OF D MAJOR

The chords in D Major are D, G and A7.

Accompaniment Styles

THE D SCALE IN TWO OCTAVES

FRETS 7 9 10

Prelude

Etude

CARCASSI

THIRDS IN THE KEY OF D

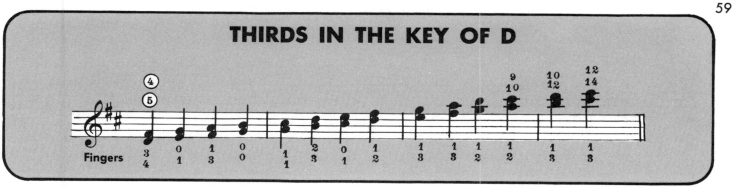

Serenade

R. de VISEE

ANDANTE IN D MAJOR

J. KÜFFNER

Sor's Etude In D Major

Moderato

Signs Appertaining To Expression and Phrasing

The Staccato: (♪♪♪ or ♪♪♪) indicate Staccato. Tones designated in this manner will be played in a disconnected style with emphasis.

♪♪♪♪ : Short lines over note indicate emphasis and individuality.

♪ ♪ ♪ : Every tone marked this way should be emphasized individually and slightly separated.

> : Accent with sudden force.

Legato (⌒): All tones will be connected and played in a flowing style.

◁ : Gradual increase of intensity or volume.

▷ : Gradual diminishing of intensity.

The Swell (◁▷): Increase and diminish volume.

Gavotte

J. S. BACH
Arr. Mel Bay

Allegro Moderato

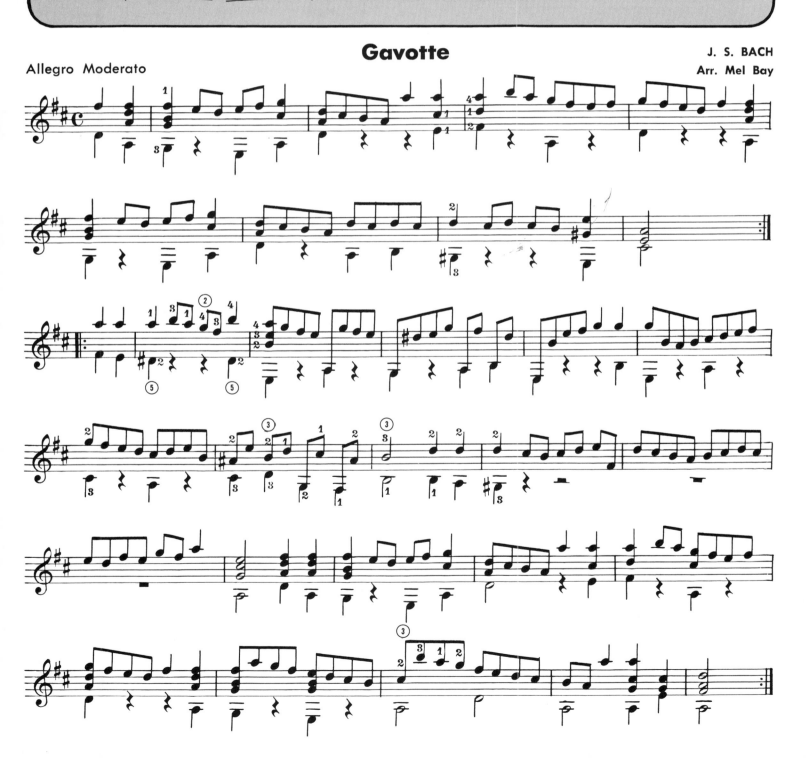

The Key of B Minor
(Relative to D Major)
THE B MINOR SCALES

Etude in B Minor

Bourree
(IN B MINOR)

JOHANN KRIEGER
1651-1735

THE CHORDS IN THE KEY OF B MINOR

The chords in the key of B Minor are Bm, Em, and F#7.

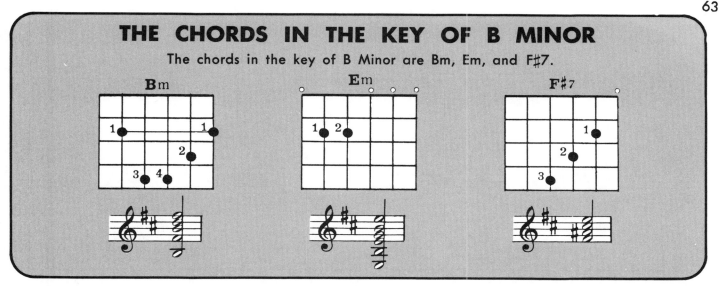

Accompaniment Styles

Love Song

Prelude in B Minor

Allegretto

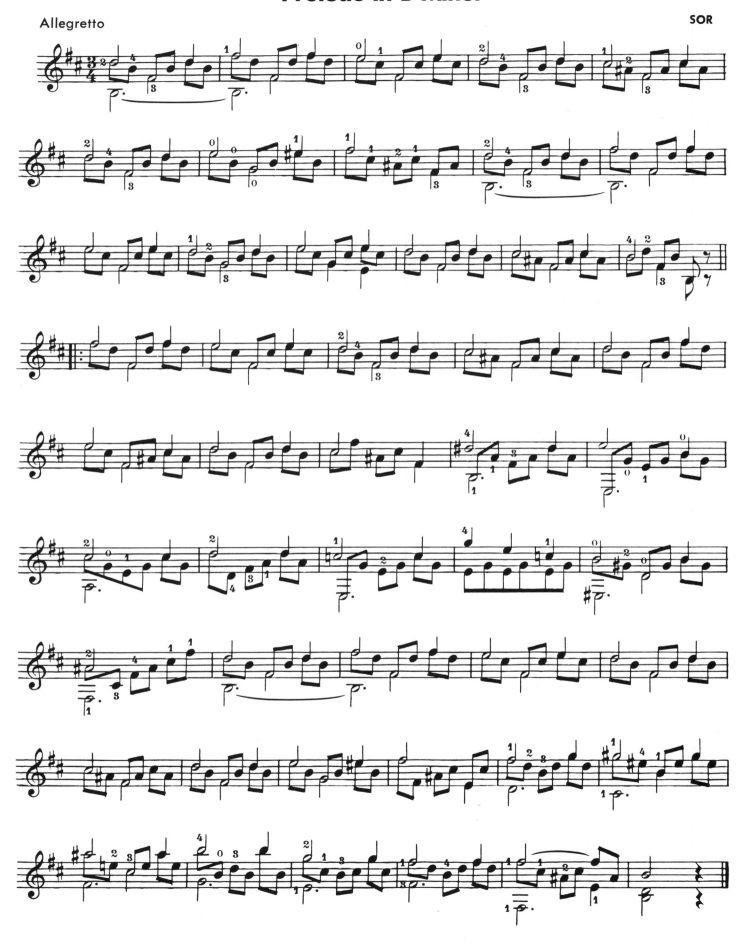

GRACE NOTES

Grace notes are small-sized notes, which subtract their value from the note they precede.

The technical term for the grace note is Appoggiatura.

The grace note will be crossed at the end and will be played the same as slurs.

When the grace note is on a different string from the principal note, pick them separately.

EXAMPLES 1 and 2

The Trill

When a note alternates according to its value, very rapidly with a tone or half-tone above it the effect produced is termed the trill.

The best produced by picking the first or principal note and slurring the upper auxiliary note.

The Mordente

The Mordente is a fragment of a Trill. It is indicated by the sign: 𝆗

MORE SIGNS

Tenuto (^): Hold the tone its full value.

Rubato: Stolen from one tone and added to a tone preceding.

Luft Pause (//): An exaggerated pause. Uusally follows a note that is held by a hold sign, (fermata). Example: 𝄐 //

The Comma (**,**) is used sometimes to indicate an interruption in the flow of tone.

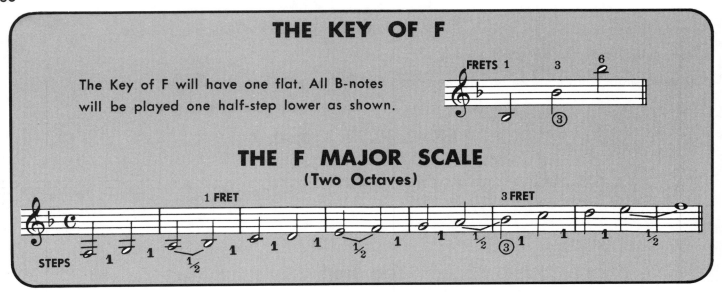

THE KEY OF F

The Key of F will have one flat. All B-notes will be played one half-step lower as shown.

THE F MAJOR SCALE
(Two Octaves)

A Daily Study

March Majestic

Arr. by Mel Bay

D. S. al Fine (Dal Segno al Fine) Go back to the sign 𝄋 and play to **Fine** (the end).

Triplet Etude

In the following triplet etude employ the following Right Hand patterns: imi, mim, mam, ama.

The Happy Farmer

THE CHORDS IN THE KEY OF F

The three chords in the key of F are F, B-flat, and C7.

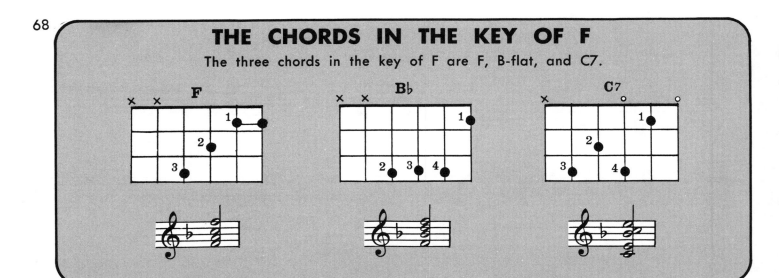

Accompaniment Styles

Common Time

Three-Four Time

Two-Four Time

Melody in F

GUITAR SOLO
Moderato

RUBENSTEIN-BAY

Minuet from Don Juan

MOZART

The Music Box

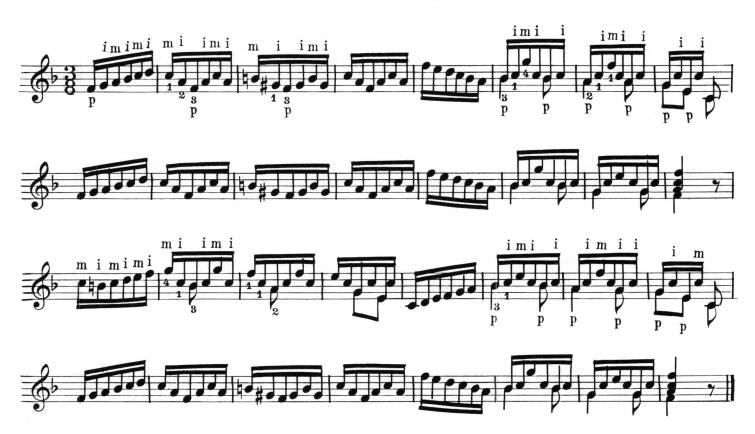

ANDANTE

F. CARULLI

THE KEY OF D MINOR

(Relative to F Major)

The D Minor Scales

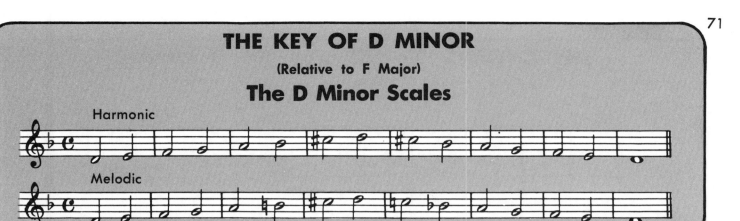

Etude in D Minor

March Slav

TSCHAIKOWSKY

THE CHORDS IN THE KEY OF D MINOR

The three principal chords in the key of D minor are:

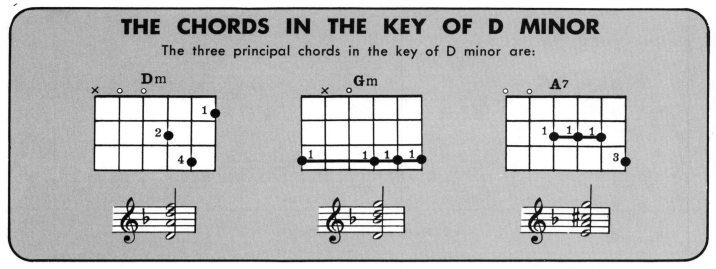

Accompaniment Styles

Common Time

Three-Four Time

Two-Four Time

Balkan Skies

GIULIANI

Andantino

Caprice

CARCASSI

74

THE KEY OF A

The key of A will have three sharps. (F#, C#, and G#.)

It will be identified by this signature:

The notes affected by the above signature will be played as shown:

Frets

THE A SCALE

Daily Drill

Taranto

CARCASSI

THE CHORDS IN THE KEY OF A

The three principal chords in the key of A are A, D, and E7

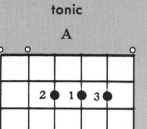
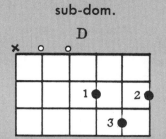
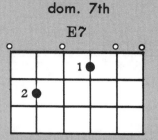

tonic — A (sub-dom.) — D (dom. 7th) — E7

THE MUSICAL NOTATION OF THE CHORDS

A — D — E7

Accompaniment Styles

Prelude

See the "MEL BAY FOLIO OF CLASSIC GUITAR SOLOS"

The Speedway

Fast

The Happy Guitarist

GUITAR SOLO

Allegretto

Maria

GUITAR SOLO

Arr. by Mel Bay

Andante

ANTON DIABELLI

See "MEL BAY'S DELUXE ALBUM OF CLASSIC GUITAR MUSIC"

THE KEY OF F# Minor

(Relative to A Major)

Two F# Minor Scales

Harmonic

Melodic

Exercise

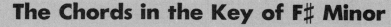

The Chords in the Key of F# Minor

The chords in the Key of F# Minor are F#m, Bm, and C#7.

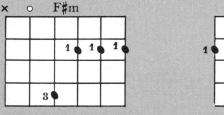
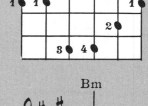
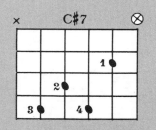

⊗ = DEADENED STRING — Kill the sound of the string with the unused part of the left hand. (See the MEL BAY CHORD SYSTEM for further explanation).

Accompaniment Styles

See "MEL BAY'S DELUXE ALBUM OF CLASSIC GUITAR MUSIC"

MORE CHROMATIC SIGNS

Up to this point we have studied and used the Sharp (#), the Flat (♭), and the Natural (♮). The student is familiar by now with their function. We now introduce the Double-Sharp and the Double-Flat.

    x = Double-Sharp. A Double-Sharp will raise the sound of a tone **two frets**.

    ♭♭ = Double Flat. A Double-Flat will lower the sound of a tone **two frets**.

A natural will cancel all sharps, flats, double-sharps and **double-flats**. If a note has been double-sharped or double flatted, the return to one sharp or flat will require a natural sign followed by the desired sharp or flat.

Example: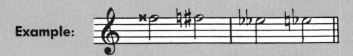

Major To Relative Minor Etude

SIX-EIGHT TIME

This sign  indicates six-eight time.

6 — beats per measure
8 — type of note receiving one beat

An Eighth-note ♪ = one beat, a quarter-note ♩ = two beats and a dotted quarter note ♩. = three beats, a sixteenth-note ♬ = ½ beat.

Six-eight time consists of two units containing three beats each.

It will be counted: with the accents on beats one and four.

1 - 2 - 3 - 4 - 5 - 6

Don Quixote

AGUADO

THE DOTTED EIGHTH NOTE

A Dotted Eighth-note is equal to

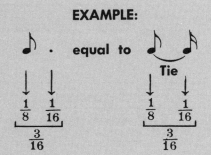

EXAMPLE:

♪. equal to ♪ ♪
Tie

$\frac{1}{8}$ $\frac{1}{16}$ $\frac{1}{8}$ $\frac{1}{16}$
$\frac{3}{16}$ $\frac{3}{16}$

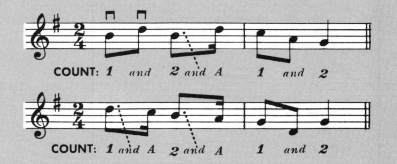

COUNT: *1 and 2 and A   1 and 2*

COUNT: *1 and A 2 and A   1 and 2*

The Little Elf

Andantino

CARULLI

Adventure

Andantino

CARULLI

THE NOTES ON THE THIRD STRING

The notes on the third (G) string are located as shown:

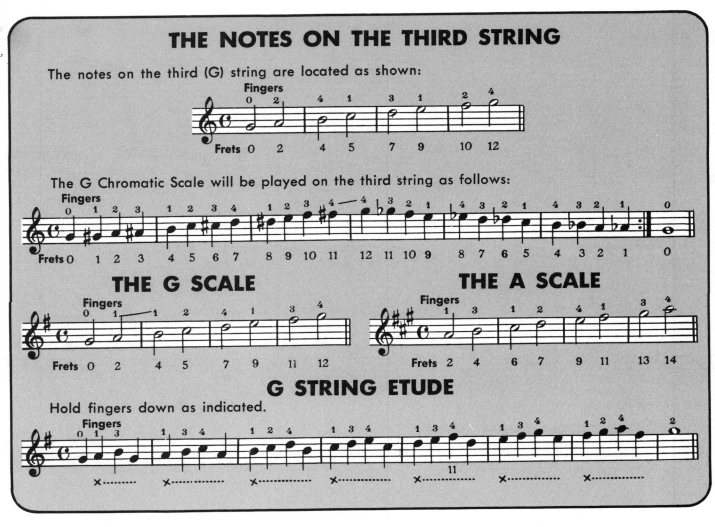

The G Chromatic Scale will be played on the third string as follows:

THE G SCALE

THE A SCALE

G STRING ETUDE

Hold fingers down as indicated.

Venetian Nights

GUITAR SOLO

M. CARCASSI
Arr. by MEL BAY

Moderato

FINE

D. C. al Fine

Prelude in A Major

Andante

SOR

See Mel Bay's

"Guitar Finger Board Harmony"

THE NOTES OF THE FOURTH STRING

A TABLE OF NOTES ON THE
FIRST, SECOND, THIRD AND FOURTH STRINGS

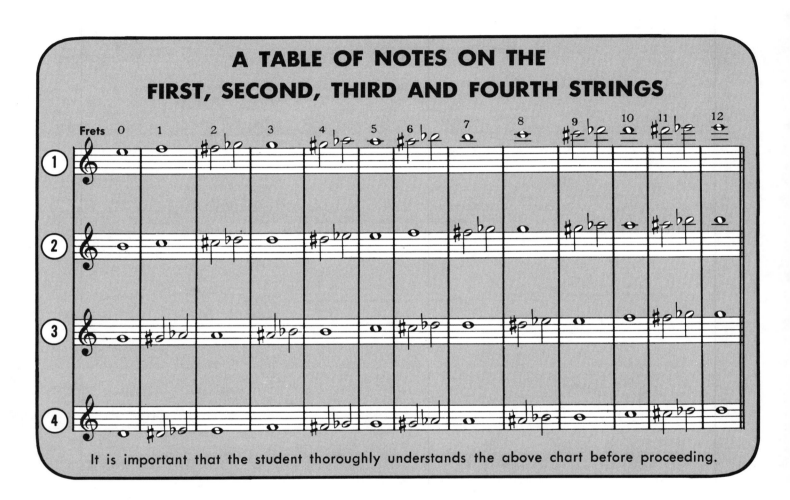

It is important that the student thoroughly understands the above chart before proceeding.

The Lido

GIULIANI

Recreation

M. GIULIANI

Allegro

The Key of E Major

The key of E will have four sharps. All F, C, G, and D notes will be sharped.

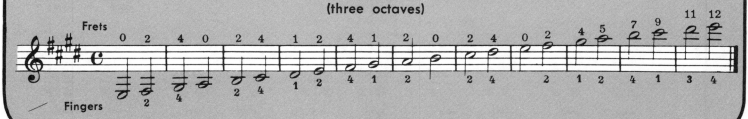

THE E MAJOR SCALE

(three octaves)

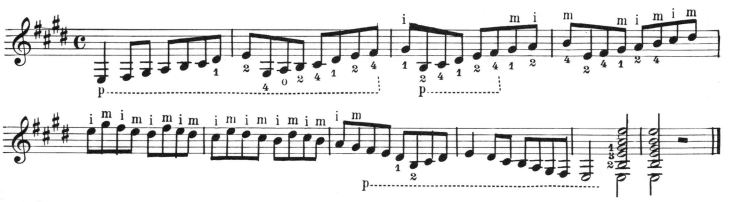

Etude

Triplet Etude in E Major

MEL BAY

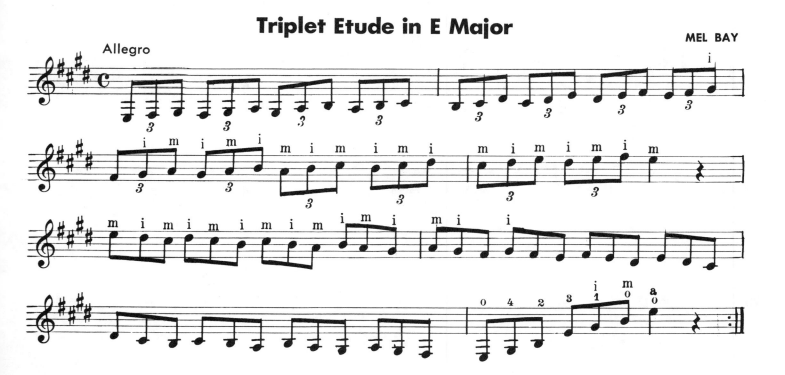

THE CHORDS IN THE KEY OF E MAJOR

THE CHORDS IN THE KEY OF E MAJOR ARE: E, A AND B7.

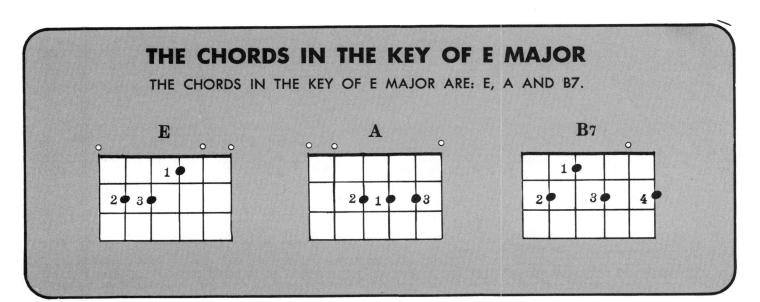

Accompaniment Styles

Prelude

Waltz in E

CARULLI

Da Capo al Fine

Frolic

SOR

Rondo in E Major

Spanish Waltz

Soliloquy

Allegretto

Soliloquy (Cont.)

Step Lively

D.C. al Fine

ANDANTE

MOZART

Prelude

Bohemian Waltz

MEL BAY

✗ = Double sharp (see page 33)

F Double
Sharp

HARMONICS

Harmonics are produced by placing the finger of the left hand directly over certain frets pressing very lightly stopping the open string vibrations.

They are produced at the 12th, 7th, 4th and 3rd frets.

Barely touch the strings at any of the above frets quickly removing the finger as soon as the string has been struck. (Teacher should demonstrate)

Harmonics will be designated by the abbreviations: Har. 12, Har. 7, Har. 5, and Har. 4 placed over or under the note to be treated in this manner.

Harmonics are written an octave lower than they sound.

Table of Harmonics

Exercise

Chime Bells

GUITAR SOLO
(All notes in Harmonics)

(A Study in Harmonics)

Artificial Harmonics

Artifical Harmonics will enable the guitarist to play all notes on the guitar harmonically. They are performed in the following manner.

1. Place the finger of the left hand on the note desired.

2. Place the index finger of the right hand lightly on the string of desired note 12 FRETS ABOVE NOTE TO BE PLAYED.

3. Pluck the string quickly with the Right Hand Thumb stopping the tone with the pointed index finger.

Example

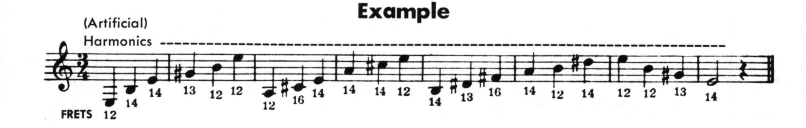

THE POSITIONS

The next goal of the student will be the complete mastery of all positions.

The material contained in this book will help the student attain that goal.

Our first chapter deals with the SECOND POSITION.

The SECOND POSITION extends from the second to the fifth frets.

In the SECOND POSITION:

> The first finger will cover the second fret.
>
> The second finger will cover the third fret.
>
> The third finger will cover the fourth fret.
>
> The fourth finger will cover the fifth fret.

Notes in the Second Position

The major keys played in the Second position are G, D, and A.

There will be **no open strings**.

Second Position Etude Number One (Key of D)

(Use 1st and 2nd R.H. Fingers Throughout)

Repeat the above employing the 2nd and 3rd R.H. Fingers.

(m)   (a)

The Major Chords in the Second Position

The Minor Chords in the Second Position

The Seventh Chords in the Second Position

Etude in the Key of G
(Second Position)

MEL BAY

Repeat the above using the 2nd and 3rd R.H. Fingers.
(m)   (a)

SEE THE MEL BAY DELUXE ALBUM OF CLASSIC GUITAR MUSIC

THE CHORDS IN THE KEY OF C

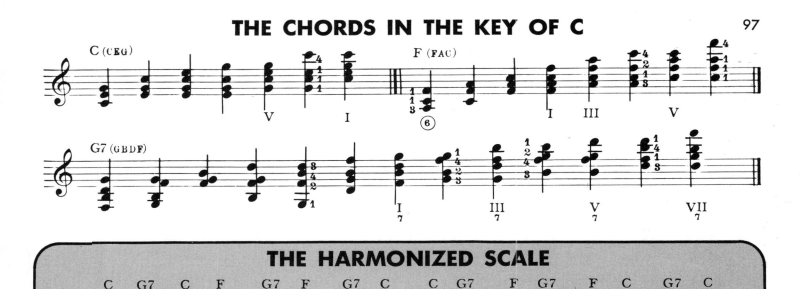

THE HARMONIZED SCALE

THE CHORDS IN THE KEY OF A MINOR

THE HARMONIZED SCALE

Sor's Waltz

CHORDS IN THE KEY OF G

*Top note of 15th fret.

THE HARMONIZED SCALE

CHORDS IN THE KEY OF E MINOR

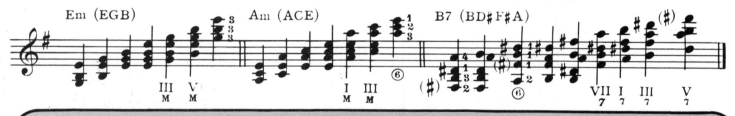

THE HARMONIZED SCALE

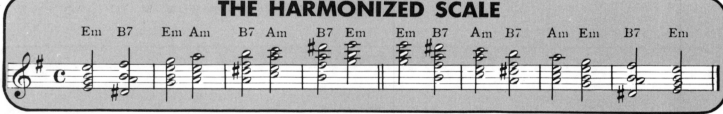

Silver Threads Among the Gold

THE CHORDS IN THE KEY OF D

THE HARMONIZED SCALE

THE CHORDS IN THE KEY OF B MINOR

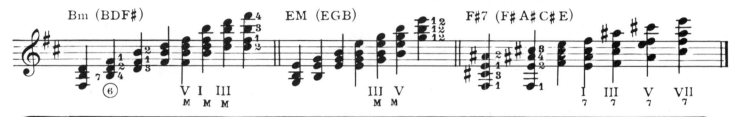

THE HARMONIZED SCALE

Rosario

THE CHORDS IN THE KEY OF A

HARMONIZED SCALE

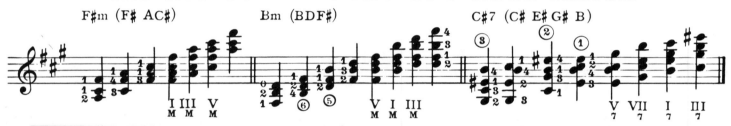

THE CHORDS IN THE KEY OF F-SHARP MINOR

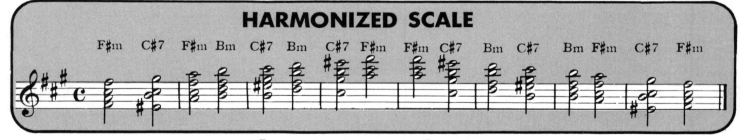

HARMONIZED SCALE

Chopin's Prelude

Arr. by MEL BAY

CHORDS IN THE KEY OF F

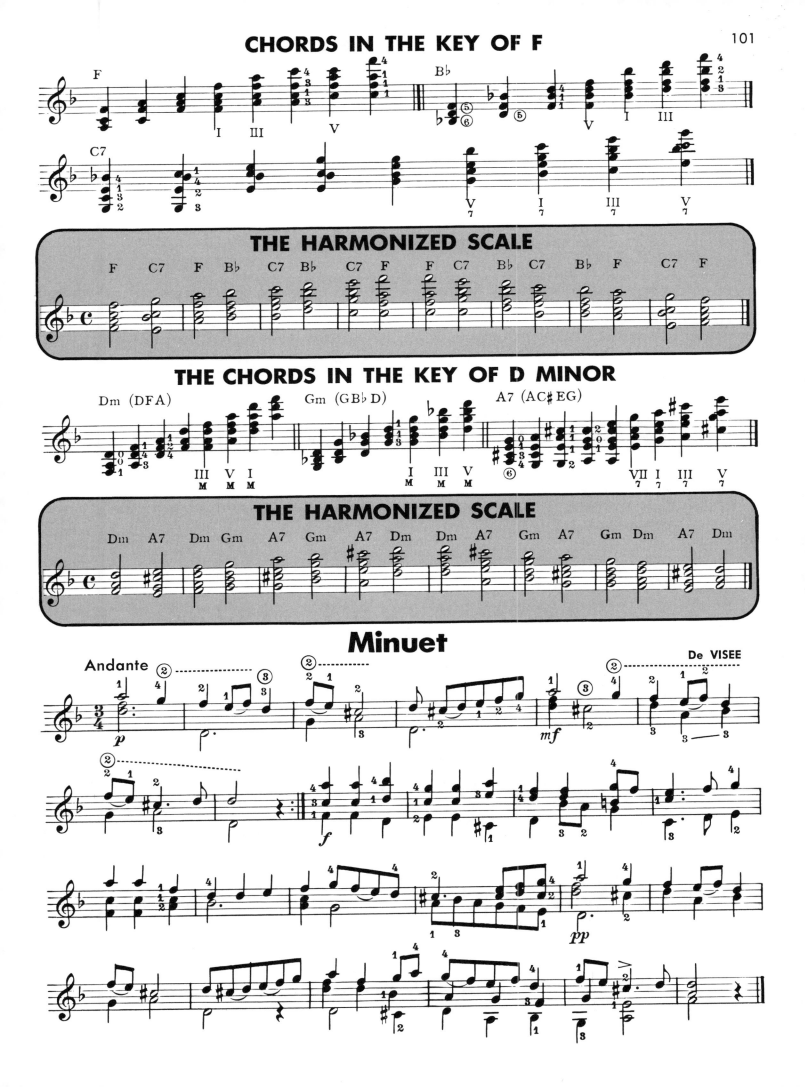

THE HARMONIZED SCALE

THE CHORDS IN THE KEY OF D MINOR

THE HARMONIZED SCALE

Minuet

De VISEE

Andante

THE KEY OF B-FLAT

The key of B-FLAT will have two flats. All B and E notes will be lowered ½ step.

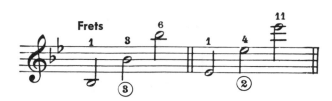

THE B-FLAT SCALE

ETUDE

THE CHORDS IN THE KEY OF B-FLAT

Bb (Bb DF)   Eb (Eb GBb)   F7 (FACEb)

MORE CHORDS IN B-FLAT MAJOR

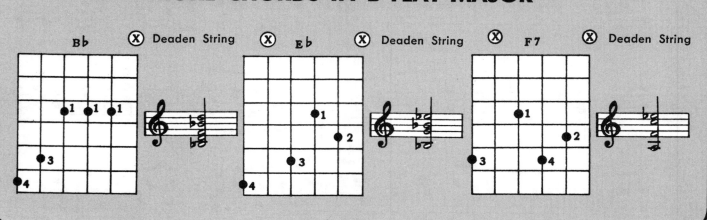

A DAILY SCALE STUDY IN B-FLAT

The Poet and the Peasant

VON SUPPE
Arr. by MEL BAY

ritard.

SEE MEL BAY'S "FLAMENCO GUITAR STYLES"

THE KEY OF G MINOR
(Relative to B-flat Major)
The key of G Minor will have the same key signature as B-flat Major.

THE G MINOR SCALES

THE CHORDS IN THE KEY OF G MINOR

Gm (G-Bb-D) Cm (C-Eb-G) D7 (D-F#-A-C)

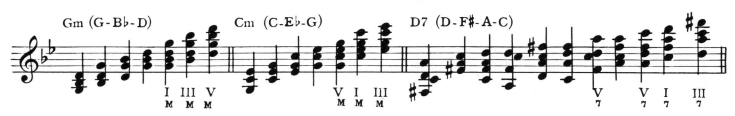

HARMONIZED SCALE

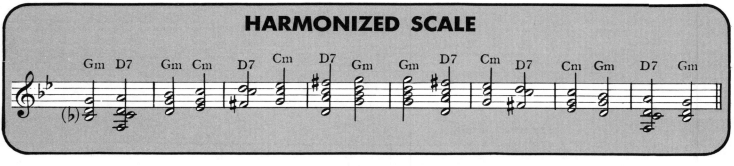

Etude in G Minor

The Key of E-Flat

The key of E♭ will have three flats. They are B♭, E♭, and A♭.

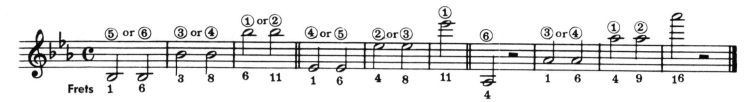

THE E FLAT MAJOR SCALE

The Third Position

The THIRD POSITION extends from the third to the sixth frets.

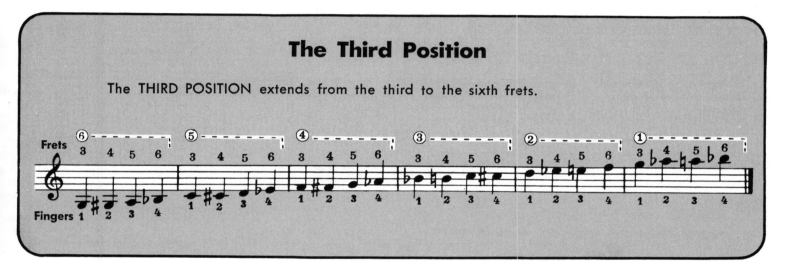

Third Position Etude One

The Chords in the Key of E-Flat

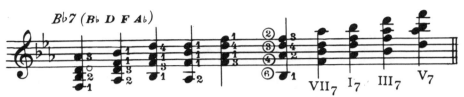

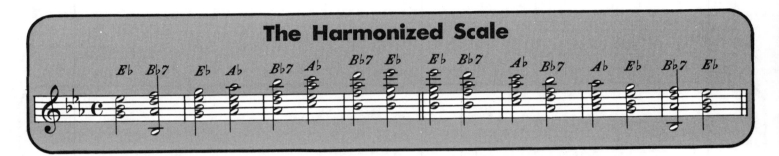

The Harmonized Scale

Alla-Breve Time

When Common time is to be played in a tempo too fast to conveniently count four beats, it is then best to count only two beats to each measure.

Each half measure will receive one beat.

This is referred to as "cut" time.

The time signature for Alla-Breve time will be a vertical line drawn through the letter C as shown: ¢

COMMON TIME

Count: 1   2   3   4

ALLA-BREVE

1   2

THE QUARTER-NOTE TRIPLET

This group of notes () is used extensively in modern music.

Three quarter-notes will be played in the same time required by two.

Caballero

PLEYEL
Arr. by MEL BAY

The Key of C Minor
(Relative to E♭ Major)

The C Minor scales will be played in the third position with the exception of the higher notes which will be played as shown.

THE C MINOR SCALES

The following etude will be in alla-breve or cut time. In grade four this type of time has been explained. When playing the quarter-note triplets, divide the measures into two beats giving each set of triplets, one beat each.

Etude in C Minor
(Third Position)

109

Prelude

C Minor Etude in the Third Position

Prelude in C Minor

The Key of A-Flat

The key of A-FLAT will have FOUR FLATS. All B, E, A and D notes will be lowered ½ step. The flatted notes are easy to remember by spelling b-e-a-d.

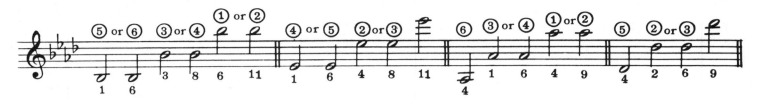

The A-Flat Scale in the Third Position

A Daily Scale Study in A-Flat

The following daily study is an excellent etude for developing finger strength and speed in good position playing. It should be played daily until the fingers tire. The amount of times should increase as the fingers become stronger. It is played entirely in the third position.

Allegro

The Chords in the Key of A Flat

The Harmonized Scale

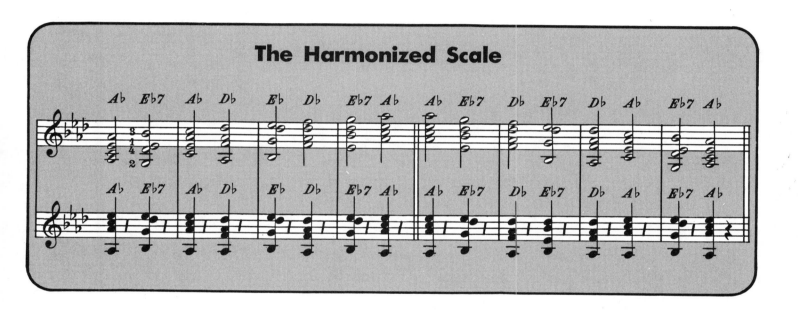

Triplet Etude in A-Flat

(Third Position)

Waltz in A Flat

JOHANNES BRAHMS
Opus 39 No. 2
Arr. by MEL BAY

See Mel Bay's
''Deluxe Guitar Arpeggio Studies''

The Key of F Minor
(Relative to A-Flat Major)
THE F MINOR SCALES

HARMONIC

MELODIC

The Chords in the Key of F Minor

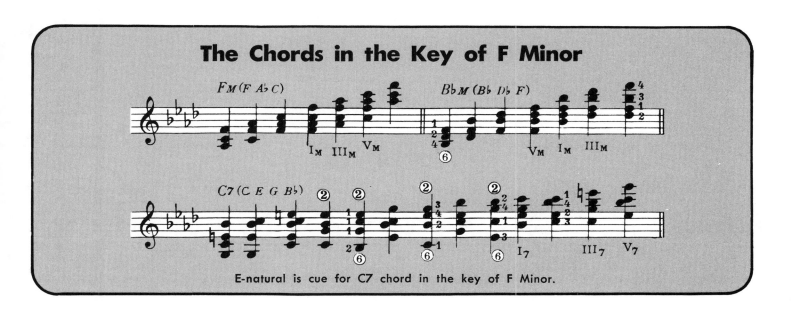

E-natural is cue for C7 chord in the key of F Minor.

Prelude in F Minor

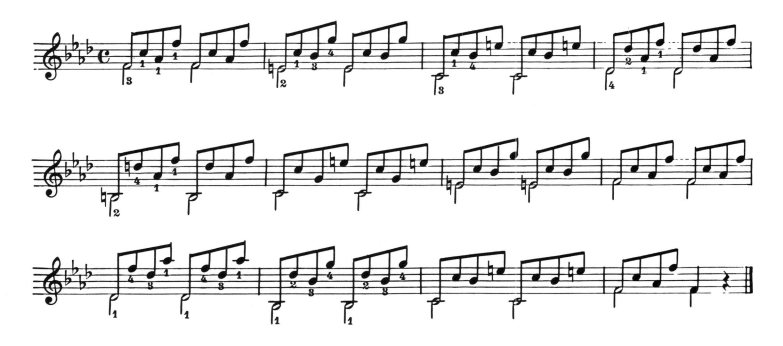

Prelude

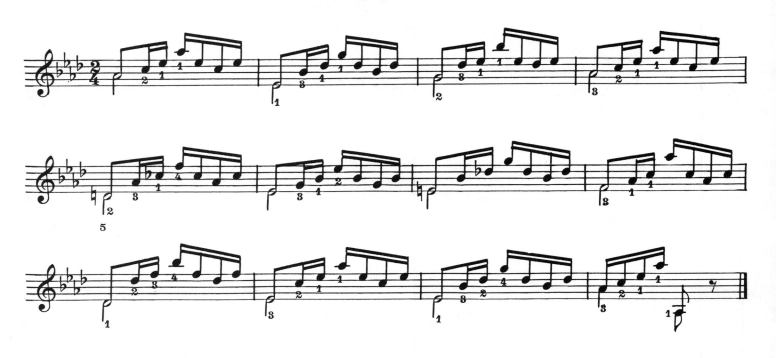

Nocturne

AGUADO

The Fourth Position

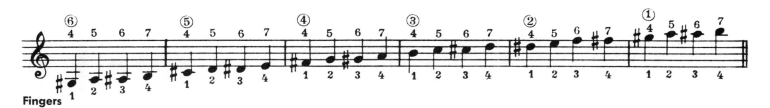

Fourth Position Exercise

WALTZ

With the exception of the open B-note*, the entire selection will be in the fourth position.

D.C.

* Designated by the zero (0)

Chords in the Fourth Position

Major Chords

Minor Chords

Seventh Chords

Diminished

Augmented

Fourth Position Etude Number One

The Key of C Sharp Minor
(Relative to E Major)

The C Sharp minor scales will be played in the Fourth Position except where shown.

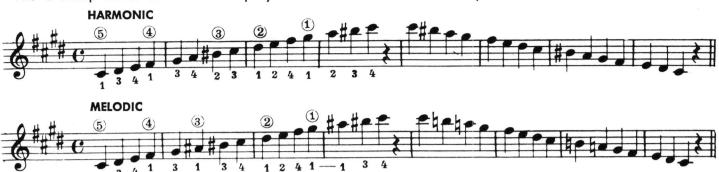

HARMONIC

MELODIC

Chords in the Key of C Sharp Minor

The Harmonized Scale

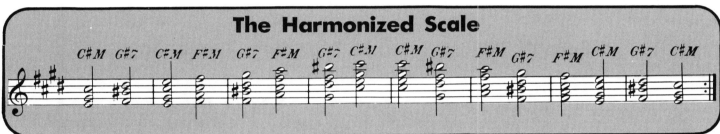

El Rey
(Fourth Position)

Allegretto

Fine

D.C. al Fine

Prelude
Opus 28 No. 20

FREDERIC CHOPIN
Arr. by MEL BAY

Largo

Fourth Position Etude Number Three
Key of A Major

Allegro

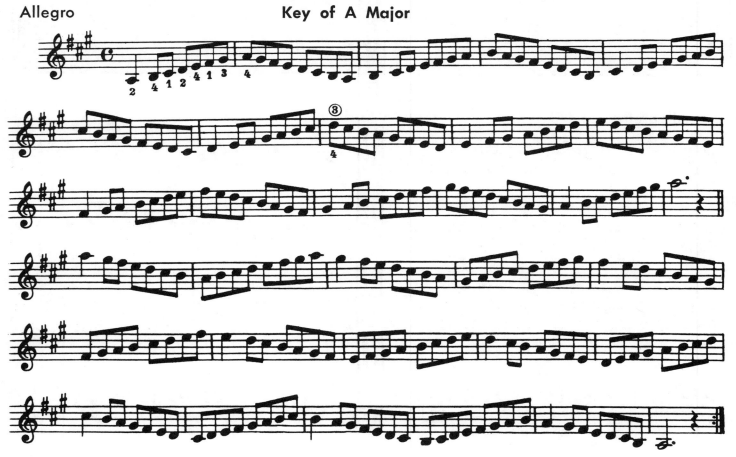

The Fifth Position

Fifth Position Exercise

The Commentator

(Fifth Position)

Guitar Solo
Allegretto

CARCASSI-BAY

ritard.

Chords in the Fifth Position

The Major Chords

The Minor Chords

The Seventh Chords

Diminished Chords

Augmented Chords

Fifth Position Etude One

The Court Jester
(Fifth Position)

GUITAR SOLO
Andantino

CARCASSI

ritard.

Fifth Position Etude Number Two

The Seventh Position

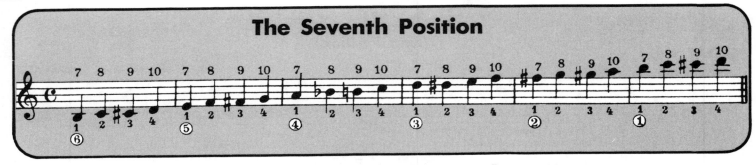

Seventh Position Etude Number One

(Repeat Using R.H. Patterns Shown at the Bottom of Page Three)

Rondo

CARCASSI

Allegretto

Chords in the Seventh Position

Major

Minor

Seventh

Diminished

Augmented

Seventh Position Etude Number Two

The Ninth Position

Ninth Position Etude

Matamoras
(Ninth Position)

Allegretto

Chords in the Ninth Position

Major

Minor

Seventh

Diminished

Augmented

Ninth Position Etude Number Two

THE KEY OF D-FLAT

The key of Db has five flats. They are Bb, Eb, Ab, Db and Gb.

The D-Flat Major Scale

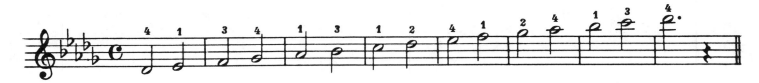

Etude in the First Position

The Chords in the Key of D-Flat

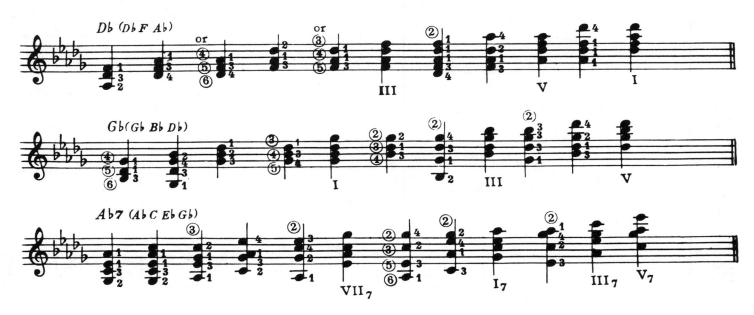

The D-Flat Scale in the Sixth Position

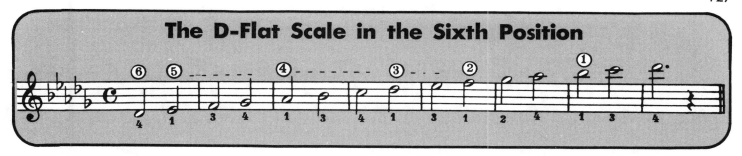

Recreation

Play the following study with a steady even beat keeping it entirely in the Sixth Position.

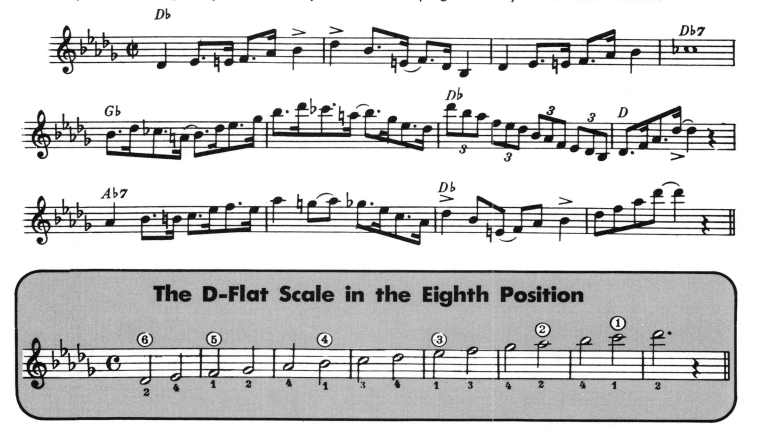

The D-Flat Scale in the Eighth Position

Eighth Position Exercise

Employ the Four Established R.H. Finger Patterns.

Prelude

Theme from the "Minute Waltz"

FREDERIC CHOPIN
Arr. by MEL BAY

Slower

THE KEY OF B-FLAT MINOR

(Relative to D-Flat Major)

The B-Minor Scales

ETUDE

The Harmonic Mode in Position

The Chords in the Key of B-Flat Minor

The Harmonized Scale

Chord Etude

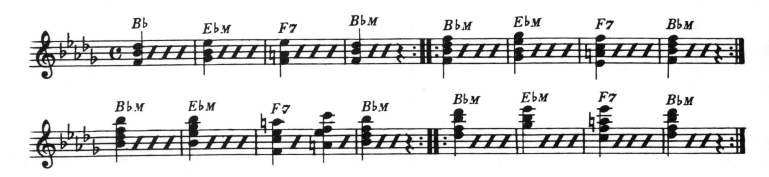

Prelude in B♭ Minor

Position Etude in B♭ Minor

Lazy Evening

Guitar Solo
Lento

MEL BAY

THE KEY OF B MAJOR

The key of B has five sharps. They are: F#, C#, G#, D# and A#.

The B Major Scale

(First Position)

Exercise in the First Position

The Chords in the Key of B

The Harmonized Scale

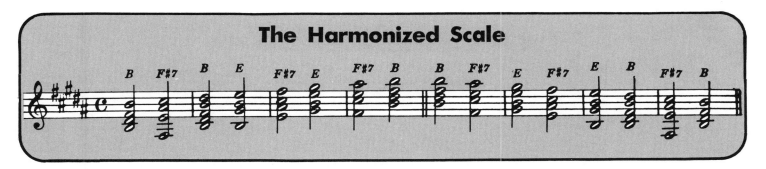

Prelude in B Major

Etude in B

For complete results play the following Etude in the First, Fourth and Sixth Positions.

THE KEY OF G-SHARP MINOR
(Relative to B Major)
The G-Sharp Minor Scales

The Chords In The Key of G-Sharp Minor

Prelude in G♯ Minor

The Keys of F-Sharp and G-Flat Major

They key of **F-Sharp** has six sharps. They are: F♯, C♯, G♯, D♯, A♯ and E♯.

The key of **G-Flat** has six flats. They are: B♭, E♭, A♭, D♭, G♭ and C♭.

THEY ARE ENHARMONIC KEYS AND WILL BE DEVELOPED TOGETHER.

The F-Sharp and G-Flat Scales in the First Position

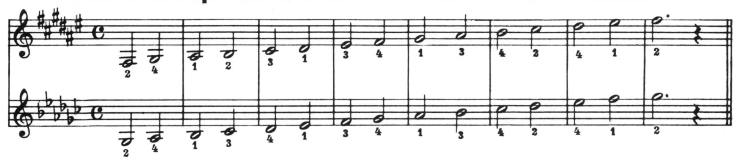

Etude in the First Position
(Play both keys)

The Chords in the Keys of F-Sharp and G-Flat Major

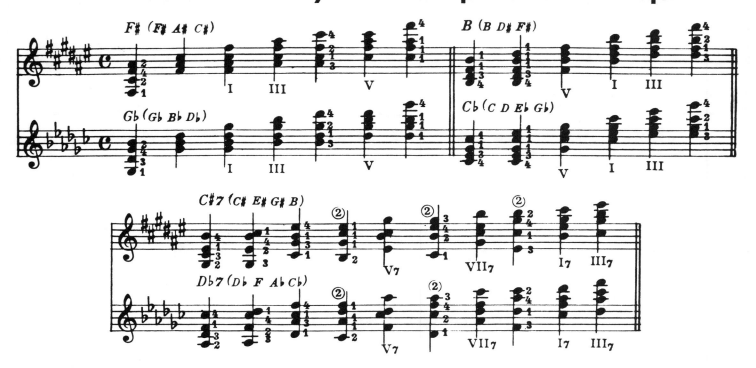

Harmonized Scales

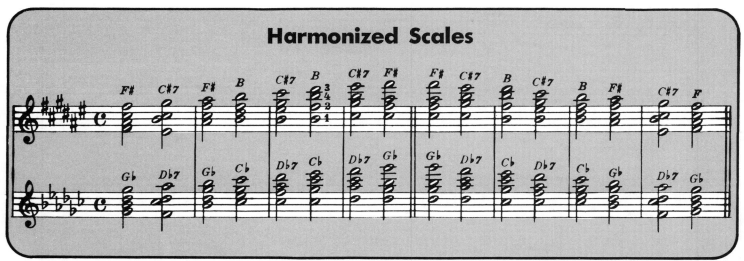

"Accompaniment Chords"

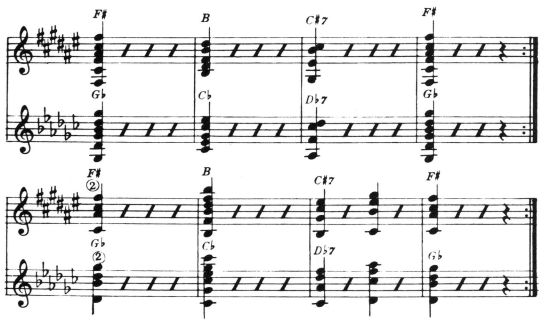

The F-Sharp and G-Flat Scales in the Sixth Position

Sixth Position Etude

The F-Sharp and G-Flat Scale in Three Octaves

The Keys of D-Sharp Minor and E-Flat Minor
(Relative to F-Sharp and G-Flat Major)

The Harmonic Mode

The Melodic Mode

CHORDS

The Harmonized Scale

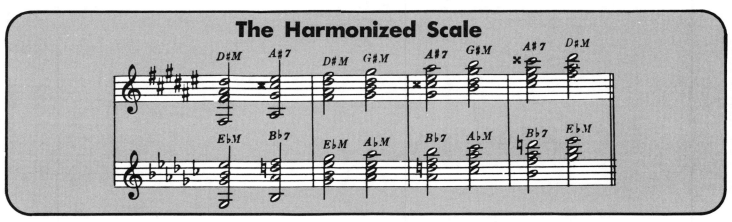

PRELUDE IN D-SHARP MINOR

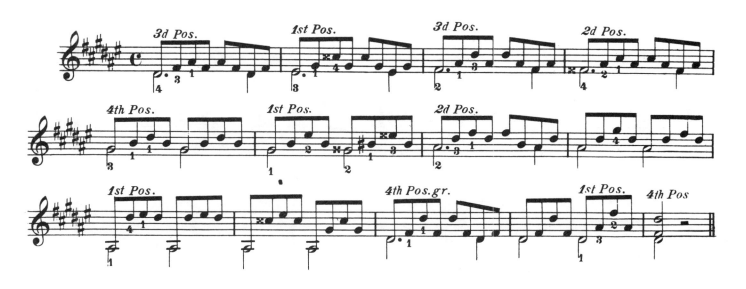

WITCHCRAFT

GUITAR SOLO
Lively

MEL BAY

Flower Song

GUITAR SOLO

LANGE
Arr. by MEL BAY

See Mel Bay's
"Johnny Smith Approach To Guitar"

WONDROUS LOVE

Tune 6th String Down To D

EARLY AMERICAN HYMN
Arr. by Bill Bay

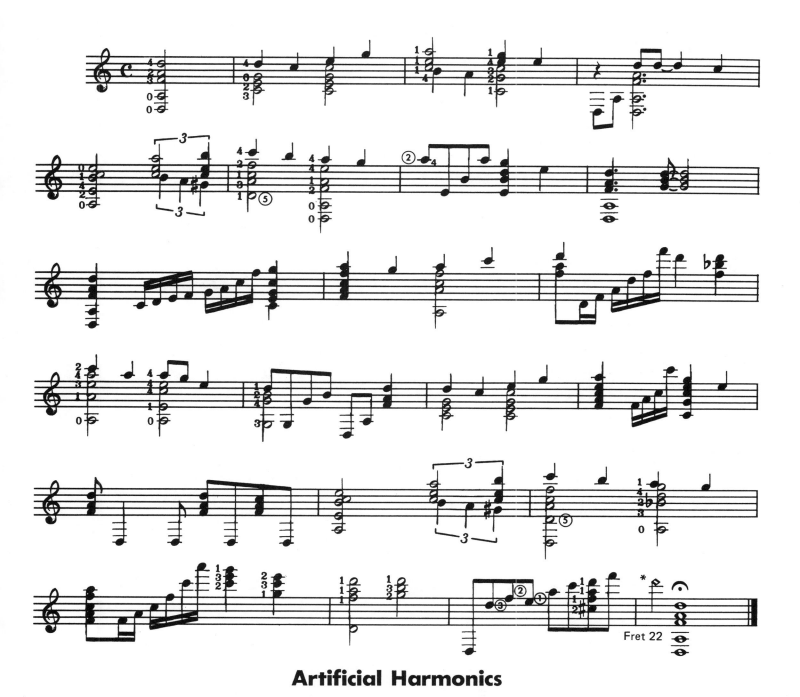

Artificial Harmonics

Artifical Harmonics will enable the guitarist to play all notes on the guitar harmonically. They are performed in the following manner.

1. Place the finger of the left hand on the note desired.

2. Place the index finger of the right hand lightly on the string of desired note 12 FRETS ABOVE NOTE TO BE PLAYED.

3. Pluck the string quickly with the Right Hand Thumb stopping the tone with the pointed index finger.

BLESSED ASSURANCE

Tune 6th String Down To Low D

FANNY CROSBY
Arr. by Bill Bay

To A Wild Rose

EDWARD MACDOWELL
Arr. by MEL BAY

With simple tenderness
Andante

LET ALL MORTAL FLESH KEEP SILENCE

Advent Hymn
Arr. By Bill Bay

Tune 6th
String to D

(Hold chord)

cadenza

ritard

(Pick chord close to bridge)